CW01085019

Lynne Harne is a lesbian mothe[...]
has been a member of Rights of [...]
the first worker for the Rights [...]
Project, between 1983 and 19[...]
lesbian mothers' experiences o[...]
published a number of articles on lesbian mothers in relation
to the law. She currently works as a part-time lecturer at the
University of Westminster teaching Women's Studies, Women
and Social Policy, and Lesbian Studies, and as a freelance
researcher and writer. She is the editor, with Elaine Miller, of
All the Rage: Reasserting Radical Lesbian Feminism (The
Women's Press, 1996).

Rights of Women, founded in 1975, is a feminist organisation
which informs women of their rights and promotes their
interests in relation to the law. The Rights of Women Lesbian
Custody Project, now the Lesbian Parenting and the Law
Project, was founded in 1982 and produced the ground-
breaking report 'Lesbian Mothers on Trial' (1984),
documenting the discrimination that lesbian mothers then
faced from the legal system. In 1986 it produced the *Lesbian
Mothers' Legal Handbook*, published by The Women's Press,
which, now completely revised and updated, has become this
book. Since then Rights of Women has continued to advise
lesbian parents and promote their legal interests, including
rights of access to donor insemination, fostering and adoption rights, and the rights of lesbians involved in co-parenting.

Also edited by Lynne Harne from The Women's Press:

All the Rage: Reasserting Radical Lesbian Feminism (1996)
with Elaine Miller

LYNNE HARNE AND RIGHTS OF WOMEN

Valued Families

The Lesbian Mothers' Legal Handbook

NEW EDITION
FULLY REVISED AND UPDATED

First published as *Lesbian Mothers' Legal Handbook* by The Women's Press, 1986
A member of the Namara Group
34 Great Sutton Street, London EC1V 0DX

New edition 1997

British Library Cataloguing-in-Publication Data
A catalogue record for this book is available from the British Library

ISBN 0 7043 4517 X

Typeset in 10/12pt Sabon by Intype London Ltd
Printed and bound in Great Britain by Caledonian International

To all lesbian parents

ACKNOWLEDGEMENTS

There are many women who helped in the development and writing of this book – members of the Rights of Women Policy Group, the workers' collective, and others who contributed their skills and expertise. We are particularly grateful to Pam Alldred, Lucy Anderson, Gill Butler, Linda Diggin, Margaret Greenfields, Sarah Maguire, Stephanie McKeon, Jill Radford, Catherine Rayner, Lisa Saffron, Jean Smith, Haema Sundram and Elizabeth Woodcraft.

Most important, we wish to thank all those lesbian parents and their children who contributed their experiences and without whom this book could not have been written.

CONTENTS

INTRODUCTION

There are now far more lesbians openly raising children than at any time in the past. Many lesbians are choosing to have children through donor insemination, and the opportunity for lesbians to foster or adopt children has become a reality. Coming out as a lesbian no longer means that the courts automatically regard a mother as unsuitable to bring up her children, and lesbian co-parents can now receive legal recognition of their parenting role.

This positive situation has been brought about not only by the changing social attitudes of the past decade but also by many years of lesbian and feminist campaigning. Lesbian mothers, feminist legal workers and researchers have all contributed to changing the situation from one in which a court in 1978 believed that being brought up by a lesbian mother would permanently 'scar' the children, to the current situation where lesbian co-parents are refused legal aid representation for joint residence order applications because it is such an uncontroversial issue. Psychological research is now available to demonstrate that which we have long known – being brought up by lesbian parents can be positively beneficial for children.

But there is no room for complacency. The position of lesbian parents is inextricably connected with the way society generally views families headed by women. For many, the 'ideal' family in Britain is still regarded as the heterosexual nuclear family.

In recent years both lesbian and lone-parent heterosexual

mothers have been targeted by political leaders and special interest groups (especially but not exclusively right wing) who are eager to reassert traditional fatherhood roles and male authority within families. Women-headed families – frequently referred to as 'families without fathers' – have been blamed for a number of social problems, and even child-centred legislation such as the recent Children Act 1989 has been used to extend 'fathers' rights' in the name of the best interests of the child. These ideological factors and Government policy on cutting public expenditure resulted in the Child Support Act 1991. Under the Act, women dependent on state benefits must authorise the pursuit of biological fathers for child maintenance, even if the father has never known the child. This has created increasing problems for families headed by women, be they lesbian or heterosexual. Drastic cuts in legal aid provision have also meant that it has become increasingly difficult for many women to gain legal representation for family matters through the courts.

This book looks at the impact of the law and social policy on lesbian parenting in recent years and provides legal advice and information relevant to lesbian mothers, co-parents and anyone considering becoming a lesbian parent. The information provided will also be useful to legal advisors, lecturers and students of law, social workers and social policy workers.

Part One explores the changing legal and social position of lesbian mothers and the change in psychological attitudes to lesbian parenting and describes recent court cases involving lesbian mothers. Part Two contains advice and strategies for lesbian parents facing a range of legal situations. This includes obtaining appropriate legal advice and representation, strategies on divorce and separation, domestic violence, immigration issues, donor insemination, co-parenting, guardianship, and adoption and fostering. Included throughout the book are first-hand accounts of lesbian parents' experiences, both negative and positive, of raising their 'valued families'. The lesbian mothers whose experiences are quoted in this book were approached and interviewed by the editor specifically for this book.

The book also contains useful appendices, a glossary

defining the legal terms used throughout, and resources, including contact organisations and suggestions for further reading.

Valued Families is based upon current law in England and Wales and excludes Scottish law, which is different in many respects.

PART 1

The changing legal and social position

CHAPTER 1

LESBIAN MOTHERS UP
AGAINST THE LAW

Attacks on lesbian parenting

Lesbians have a long history of raising children, although prior to the 1970s many women had to remain silent about being lesbians and their role as mothers. Some had to 'wait out' their marriages until the children were grown up and custody was no longer a problem before they felt safe about coming out as lesbians. Very few of the other women who were not locked into marriage but were raising children as 'aunties' were able to live openly as lesbians.[1]

During the 1970s some women with children began to identify openly and positively as lesbians, and others began to seek ways to have or raise children outside of relationships with men. Especially following the 1974 lesbian conference at the University of Kent, Canterbury, lesbian mothers became increasingly visible both inside and outside the women's liberation movement.

One consequence of this increasing visibility and confidence of lesbian mothers was that during the 1970s a number of lesbians who had been married or living with men became involved in legal custody battles for their children. In 1975, as a result of a number of anti-lesbian custody judgments, Action for Lesbian Parents was formed:

> We were a small but very active group. We formed a telephone link for isolated lesbian mothers, and for those going through the courts. We gave talks, set up a symposium, and responded to pressures from solicitors and barristers to

3

find evidence showing how children fared psychologically being raised by lesbians. We became involved with radical British and American psychologists to produce this 'evidence', and there were even pieces in the Sunday papers about how our children grow up 'normal' (as the media saw it).[2]

Action for Lesbian Parents also campaigned around the issue of lesbians obtaining access to donor insemination. In 1978 the *London Evening News* ran an 'exposé' on lesbians gaining artificial insemination by donor through a Harley Street doctor. Action for Lesbian Parents participated in a successful sit-in at the newspapers offices for the right of reply. In the same year a small group of lesbians, unwilling to depend on a largely prejudiced and expensive medical profession to provide donor insemination, set up the first self-insemination group involving a group of gay men who were willing to be donors.

By the early 1980s support and campaigning networks of lesbian mothers existed in different parts of the UK. Despite the campaigning work, discrimination against lesbian mothers continued, particularly in custody disputes. After a national conference organised specifically around the issue of lesbian custody in early 1983, Rights of Women (ROW) set up the Lesbian Custody Project (LCP).

With funding from the Greater London Council and a paid research and advice worker, the project set out to research the discrimination experienced by lesbian mothers in custody disputes (both by a review of the court cases and a survey of individuals), give legal advice to lesbian mothers and lawyers, and support the psychological research already being undertaken to help lesbian mothers involved in such disputes. The research was carried out between 1983 and 1984.

DISCRIMINATION AGAINST LESBIAN MOTHERS IN CUSTODY DISPUTES 1976–1984

Review of the court cases

The project conducted a review of the few reported and appeal cases between 1976 and 1984, which demonstrated a depressing saga of discriminatory attitudes against lesbian mothers by the judiciary. Despite the legal principle that the welfare of the child should have been 'the first and paramount consideration',[3] these cases showed that decisions focused on lesbianism as the dominating factor as to why a mother should not have custody, rather than examining the quality and care of the parental relationships. This was in contrast to the judiciary's treatment of heterosexual mothers involved in similar disputes during the same period; in those cases, providing the mother already had the children living with her and they were relatively young, custody was usually awarded to her.[4]

Historically a mother's behaviour has always been considered relevant by the legal system in interpreting the welfare principle in custody disputes. Up until the late 1960s adultery was considered enough to prevent a mother from keeping her children. Lord Denning's 1962 judgment illustrated this:

> This good [good mothering] in itself is not always enough, one must remember that to be a good mother involves not only looking after the children, but making and keeping a home for them with their father ... insofar as she herself by her conduct broke up that home, she is not a good mother. (Re L (infant) 1962)

By the 1970s, however, a number of appeal judgments demonstrated that a heterosexual mother's conduct in this respect was no longer considered relevant, presumably because in most cases it was considered that she would remarry and consequently a male presence in the family would continue. Moreover, the Matrimonial Causes Act 1973 considerably simplified procedures to end unhappy marriages, leading to an increasing number of women applying for divorce and hence custody of their children. Inevitably the courts were forced to acknowledge the growing shift towards social acceptability of lone parents as a result of relationship breakdown, and to a large extent began to ignore the conduct of the woman in determining with whom the children should live.

In contrast, in lesbian custody cases a mother's sexual identity, politics, and the lack of men's presence in lesbian families to provide 'appropriate' male role models became key elements. Some of the earliest judgments referred to the possibility of children being 'blemished', or permanently 'scarred' if they were brought up by lesbians (*S v S* 1978). Lesbianism was described as 'deviant' (*S v S* 1978), 'devious' (*Re P* 1982), 'unnatural' (*E v E* 1980), 'abnormal' and 'unstable' (*G v D* 1983). Many of these judgments were based on the predominant belief at the time that lesbians, because they were asserting an autonomous sexual identity, somehow took on the worst aspects of male sexual behaviour. It was assumed that they were oversexed and would sexually abuse children.[5]

Judges were also concerned about awarding custody to lesbian mothers because it might be seen as showing public approval of lesbianism and this could herald 'the decay of society'[6] and would not be in 'the public interest' (*Re P* 1982). There was also an emphasis on the possibility of children being teased by their peers, of their being 'subject to social embarrassment and hurt' (*S v S* 1978) or 'subject to taunts' (*E v E* 1980).

Despite these pronouncements, some lesbian mothers did gain custody at appeal, largely because the father was unable to provide suitable accommodation (*W v W* 1976) or care for the child (*Re P* 1982) or because the children refused to live with him (*G v D* 1983). Not surprisingly, however, the judges in these cases did speak of the desirability of children growing up in what they regarded as 'normal families', with a 'father and mother or mother substitute' (*W v W* 1976, *G v D* 1983). In a significant appeal judgment in 1983 the court held that:

the mere fact of this homosexual way of life on the part
of the mother is not, in itself, a reason for refusing to give
her control of her children, although ... of course it is a
factor that one has to take into account and think about
very hard. (*G v D* (1983))

Survey of individuals

Since the vast majority of disputed cases were not reported
in the legal journals or never got as far as an appeal, in 1983
the Lesbian Custody Project also undertook a survey of the
experiences of 36 women involved in such disputes. It found
that many lesbian mothers were affected by the legal advice
they initially received, even before any court hearing. Ignorance of the issues or prejudice against lesbians by solicitors
and barristers meant that a number of lesbian mothers were
advised to give up their children because they were told that
they had no hope of winning or that their children might be
taken into care. Others were advised to come to unsatisfac-
tory agreements about access and maintenance or to agree to
joint custody (shared residence and decision-making between
both parents) in order to avoid a court hearing. Following
this the Project worked to find and educate sympathetic
lawyers about the issues involved.

The survey also found that where mothers did get as far
as a court hearing and a welfare report was ordered, the
attitude of the court welfare officer was crucial in the outcome
of the case. Of those lesbian mothers who had hearings,
many found that a prurient interest was taken in their sexual
practices by the court. They described being made to feel like
criminals. They felt that the court was punishing them for
being lesbians rather than looking at their relationship with
their children. A few lesbian mothers were awarded custody,
but with conditions – for example, never to see the children
with their partner present, or being prohibited from engaging
in feminist activism. Even though a number of mothers had
experienced violence or sexual abuse at the hands of the

father, overwhelmingly the focus of the court was on the mother's behaviour rather than the father's.

Most significantly, the survey found that of those lesbian mothers who lost custody at a court hearing, all had had their children living with them for a substantial period of time and the vast majority of the children had been under the age of eleven.

POSITIVE CHANGES

By the mid-eighties the situation began to change. This was helped by psychological research undertaken in Britain which demonstrated that children were not 'harmed' by being brought up by lesbian mothers.[7] This research (described in more depth in Chapter Three) began to be frequently used by expert witnesses in court and became significant in winning a number of cases.

The Lesbian Custody Project also set up a network of feminist lawyers to which lesbian mothers involved in disputes could be referred, and it developed and delivered training workshops for solicitors and barristers on conducting custody cases. The National Association of Probation Officers (who usually act as court welfare officers) passed a resolution concerning non-discrimination on the grounds of sexuality, and the Project provided educational workshops for those training in that area.

The changed climate was also helped by the increasing visibility and organisation of lesbian mothers themselves, including some women who had had children through self-insemination and were not under threat of losing their children if they spoke out publicly. In 1985 the Project participated in a film about lesbian mothers called 'Breaking the Silence', which was shown on Channel 4 and repeated in 1987, and subsequently participated in numerous other radio and television programmes. It organised conferences and supported growing networks of lesbian mothers throughout the country, and produced a charter for combatting all forms of discrimination against lesbian parents. Additionally, the

Project's work emphasised how racism and poverty could compound the discrimination experienced by lesbian mothers.

The publication of the LCP research in 1984 and the *Lesbian Mothers' Legal Handbook* in 1986 contributed to highlighting the discrimination faced by lesbians and bringing about strategies for change. By 1993, for example, one solicitor reported to the Project that over a period of four years she had only lost one case out of fifteen where a mother's sexual orientation had been raised as an issue.

The few appeal judgments that have taken place in the 1990s have also reflected this altered judicial attitude. Although a mother's lesbian relationship is still regarded as an 'important factor' in considering a child's welfare, it 'does not of itself render her unfit to have care and control of her child' (*C v C* 1991). (See Chapter Four for an overview of court decisions in the 1990s.)

ATTACKS ON LESBIAN PARENTING

Pretending families and Clause 28

During the 1980s lesbian mothers were organising around more than custody issues. Many were experiencing discriminatory attitudes towards themselves and their children in the education system. The London group Lesbians in Education focused its attention on the Inner London Education Authority (ILEA) and campaigned to get the authority to develop policies that would give recognition to 'different families' by the use of a variety of teaching resources and good practice.[8]

At the same time a right-wing backlash was building up, aimed at restoring 'traditional' family values. In 1986, a right-wing Christian family campaign was launched with an opening address entitled, 'Putting Father Back at the Head of the Table'. Its key aim was to 'make the family a central political issue', and it identified feminism as its main enemy: 'Years of militant feminism and harmful legislation like the

Equal Opportunities Act have undermined the clear biblical concept of the father.'[9]

The campaign was targeted in the first instance at ILEA and local authorities such as Haringey who were considering providing resources for schools that addressed lesbian and gay issues. The ILEA did eventually publish a resource list for teachers in 1987 which included some information sources on lesbian families; however, on the eve of publication ILEA lost its nerve, and books meant for under fives – such as *Lots of Mommies* – became listed as suitable only for 14-year-olds.[10]

In 1986 the Government had already passed a clause stating that where sex education is taught, it should encourage pupils to 'have due regard to moral considerations and the value of family life' (Education No (2) Act 1986 s. 46). The wording implicitly excluded any form of family other than heterosexual ones.

A Private Member's Bill which had been introduced in the same year by the Earl of Halsbury to 'prevent the promotion by local authorities of homosexuality as an acceptable family relationship' was first thought to be unnecessary in light of the Education No (2) Act 1986. However, by late 1987, the Government had changed its mind, because it was felt that the phrase 'family life' could be broadly interpreted to include lesbian or gay families. As a result, the draft Local Government Bill included Clause 28 of the Act, which said that local authorities should not 'intentionally promote homosexuality' or 'promote the teaching in any maintained school of the acceptability of homosexuality as a pretended family relationship' (Local Government Act 1988 s. 2(a)).

Legal opinion sought by the National Council for Civil Liberties on the meaning of this latter phrase suggested it had been included to

> emphasise Parliament's view that a homosexual family relationship is not a real family relationship. [It] appears to prohibit local authorities from advocating, either directly or indirectly, that pupils should be taught, at least as part of their curriculum, that a homosexual family relationship

is acceptable as being on a par with a heterosexual family relationship.[11]

The Lesbian Custody Project, along with many lesbian mothers, participated in the massive anti-'Clause 28' campaign. As Jill Radford reported in the Winter 1995 *Rights of Women Bulletin*:

> Shifting into public protest, lesbians involved in LCP played an active role in the wider campaign against the Clause, speaking at too many meetings to count; participating in TV discussion programmes, briefing Lords and Ladies, giving press interviews. Wearing our 'we are not pretending' badges, we marched in London and travelled with our pretending children, on the pink train ... to the Manchester march.

Nevertheless the Clause was passed in the final Act, and it meant that many schools and teachers felt that they could not openly discuss or use resources that would validate the home life of children of lesbians, even though the prohibition is on local authorities, and not on individual schools. Some schools continue to develop equal opportunities policies that aim to combat discrimination against lesbian families. Children of lesbians who attend such schools have described the positive effect this has had for them.

The Children Act 1989 and the Child Support Act 1991

The Children Act 1989 reinforced the presumption that ongoing father/child contact is in a child's best interests. The Child Support Act 1991 furthered women's dependency on men by requiring biological fathers to pay financial maintenance for both the child and the mother. Women on social security benefits face the danger that if they do not name the father to the authorities, who would then pursue him for a financial contribution, they will suffer a benefit deduction.

The effects on lesbian mothers of these and other legislative changes are discussed in Chapter Two.

The attack on access to donor insemination

In 1989, with the introduction of the Human Fertilisation and Embryology Bill, which set out to regulate new reproductive technology, right-wing politicians and religious groups led another attack against lesbians in particular and 'single' women in general, this time attempting to stop them having children through donor insemination. Although the main body of the Bill was concerned with embryology and 'test-tube babies', a number of clauses inserted during its passage through Parliament provided an opportunity to regulate and limit access to the older and more simple technique of artificial insemination by donor.

An Early Day Motion in October 1989 reflected some of the views held by supporters of the 'traditional family':

This house notes with profound concern the recent revelation that 55 lesbian couples and eight single lesbians have been impregnated by one sperm bank alone during the last three years: expresses its dismay at the ease with which these and two thousand other unmarried women who are not infertile were able to gain access to such facilities: believes such practices undermine the status of marriage, corrupt the family unit, and leave the children at grave risk of emotional harm. . .[12]

As a result of this, the Campaign for Access to Donor Insemination (CADI), with which LCP was involved, was set up to lobby for changes to the Bill. The campaign fought hard against a series of amendments raised during the committee stage of the Bill which would have prevented any 'single' women from gaining access to donor insemination through clinics. The risk of HIV infection made it particularly important that lesbians had access to sperm donors who had been properly screened, and the clinics were one means of ensuring proper screening. There was also a fear that the informal donor insemination arrangements used by self-insemination groups would be made illegal.

In 1990 the Bill became law as the Human Fertilisation and Embryology Act. In spite of an amendment referring to the fact that clinics must consider the need of any child for a father before providing donor insemination, the wording is sufficiently ambiguous to allow them to continue to provide donor insemination to lesbians and 'single' women. It was deemed impractical to legislate against informal sperm donor arrangements, although all sperm banks using frozen sperm now have to be licensed and regulated by the HFEA Authority. However, the enactment of the Child Support Act 1991 has also presented problems for women choosing to use informal self-insemination techniques (see Chapter Eight).

Attacks on fostering and adoption

Lesbian parenting also came under attack when new Government regulations and guidance for fostering and adoption were being considered following the Children Act 1989. Draft foster placement guidance issued by the Department of Health for consultation in 1990 stated that

> ... authorities and those interested in becoming foster parents must understand that an authority's duty is, unequivocally and unambiguously, to find and approve the most suitable foster parents for children who need family placement. It would be wrong arbitrarily to exclude any particular groups of people from consideration. But the chosen way of life of some adults may mean that they would not be able to provide a suitable environment for the care or nurture of a child. No one has a right to be a foster parent. 'Equal rights' and 'gay rights' policies have no place in fostering services.[13]

This represents a scarcely veiled attack on a few local authorities who had developed equal opportunities policies in the

1980s which enabled them to recruit and approve 'out' lesbians as foster or adoptive parents. Of course, for many years there have been lesbians who have fostered or adopted children as 'single' women by concealing their lesbian identity.

Protests followed, not only from groups such as LCP but also from many child-care organisations and local authorities. In the final guidance – Volume 3 Family Placements. DoH 1991 – any reference to gay rights or any particular group was omitted, and it simply stated that 'Fostering decisions must centre exclusively on the interests of the child.'

Whilst lesbians continue to be approved as foster or adoptive parents, this area of lesbian parenting remains particularly vulnerable. Fear of adverse publicity as well as discriminatory attitudes makes many fostering and adoption agencies cautious about considering lesbians as foster or adoptive parents.

In 1991, a storm of protest was orchestrated by the local press when Newcastle City Council placed a boy with disabilities with lesbian adoptive parents. In this case the foster mother went to court to oppose the placement and won. As recently as 1995, The Children Society (one of the four largest adoption agencies operating in the voluntary sector) has continued to refuse applications from lesbians and gay men wishing to foster or adopt children, justifying their decision on Christian doctrine. Nevertheless the number of lesbians fostering and adopting children is slowly growing, albeit in some cases with children who are considered 'hard to place' in 'more desirable' heterosexual families.

LEGAL RECOGNITION OF LESBIAN CO-PARENTING: AN EXAMPLE OF POSITIVE CHANGE

In contrast to the attitudes surrounding fostering and adoption, by 1994 judges had begun to recognise lesbians as co-parents through granting joint residence orders on application under section 8 of the Children Act 1989.

The Children Act enabled the legal recognition of non-biological parents. In particular it aimed to give recognition to the role of the stepfather in sharing parenting with a mother who remarried, without depriving the biological father of his legal parental status.[14] However, the Act has also enabled the legal recognition of any person who might share the care of a child living with her/him (Children Act 1989 s.10, s.12).

Joint residence orders that have been granted to lesbian couples confer the legal status of equal 'parental responsibility' on the non-biological parent as long as the child continues to live with her. It thus signifies a watershed in the struggles around lesbian parenting and the law.

The granting of such orders means that the co-parent can make decisions about a child's schooling or medical treatment when the child is with her. It also means that if the biological mother dies, the co-parent retains parental responsibility, and it is therefore much harder for the child to be removed by other biological relatives such as grandparents. Further, if the couple split up there is already legal recognition of the non-biological partner's parenting role, which would lend support for any application to a court for continuing contact with the child. (See Chapter Seven for a more detailed discussion of this area.)

A much publicised case (Re C 1994) involved a lesbian couple living in Manchester who applied for and gained a joint residence order in the High Court. One of the women had had a child through self-insemination, but both wished to share equally in its upbringing. In granting the joint residence order the judge stated that the welfare of the child was 'my first and paramount consideration, and that the evidence pointed overwhelmingly to the making of the order.' The ruling did create a furore amongst Tory MPs and the tabloid press. Emma Nicholson MP said: '. . . for a child to grow up with two lesbian mothers was neither normal nor natural', and the Daily Mail warned that the ruling 'opened the way for us to become a nation of man-hating all-female families.'[15]

Despite these reactions, the last twenty years of campaigning around lesbian parenting have meant that our social institutions can no longer deny the existence of lesbian families.

In the area of private family law, the courts are presenting an increasingly tolerant and liberal face, recognising that lesbians do not make unfit mothers simply on the basis of their sexuality – provided, of course, that they are not 'militant' and do not shout about it – and granting legal recognition to lesbian couples raising children.

The threat of legislative interference such as section 2A of the Local Government Act 1988 and the moral right lobbyists for the 'traditional' family and fathers' rights continue to have an impact on the whole area of family law, aiming to develop its direction to reinforce the ideology of the 'naturalness' of the heterosexual nuclear family and to reinforce fathers' rights in relation to children in the name of child welfare.

NOTES

1. See Sue Allen and Lynne Harne, 'Lesbian Mothers: The Fight for Child Custody' in B Cant and S Hemmings, eds, *Radical Records*, Routledge, London, 1988.

2. Sue Allen and Lynne Harne, 'Lesbian Mothers: The Fight for Child Custody'.

3. This principle was established as overriding all other claims in the Guardianship of Minors Act 1971.

4. Stephen Michael Cretney, *Principles of Family Law*, third edition, Sweet & Maxwell, London, 1979.

5. Rights of Women, *Lesbian Mothers on Trial: A Report on Lesbian Mothers and Child Custody*, Rights of Women, London, 1984.

6. Lesbian mother (anonymous), 'A Case of Heads He Wins – Tails She Loses', *Family Law Journal* 6 (1979), p230.

7. Susan Golombok, Ann Spencer and Michael Rutter, 'Children in Lesbian and Single-Parent Households: Psychosexual and Psychiatric Appraisal', *Journal of Child Psychology and Psychiatry* 124, 4 (1983), pp551–72.

8. Diane Langford and A Pfeffercorn, 'Sex Education: Who Needs It?' in *Challenging Heterosexism*, GEN (March 1987).

9. Webster, opening address 1986, quoted in Diane Langford and A Pfeffercorn, 'Sex Education: Who Needs It?', p32.

10. Diane Langford and A Pfeffercorn, 'Sex Education: Who Needs It?', p34.

11. National Council for Civil Liberties, *Section 28: A Practical Guide to the Law and Its Implications*, NCCL, London, 1989, pp13–14.

12. Hansard Order Paper no. 165. Early Day Motion no. 1234, 26 October 1989.

13. Para 16 DoH Draft Guidelines 1990.

14. A Bainham, *Children and the New Law: The Children Act 1989*, Family Law, London, 1990.

15. *Rights of Women Bulletin*, Autumn/Winter 1994.

CHAPTER 2

IN THE BEST INTERESTS OF
THE CHILDREN?

Recent family legislation and how it affects lesbian parents

Changes in family legislation over the last ten years have produced confusion and contradictions when examined from a lesbian parenting standpoint. On the one hand, there has been an apparent liberalisation of judicial attitudes towards lesbian mothers. At the same time, however, legislative changes continue to attempt to restrict autonomous motherhood.

Since the 1980s, a convergence of political forces including the religious right, family values and fathers' rights movements have generated a new discourse on the welfare of the child. The debate has now moved away from the concept that children primarily need a mother, particularly when they are young, to emphasising the need for the continuing presence of biological fathers in children's lives after divorce and separation.

Simultaneously there has been ongoing state concern about the growing number of women-headed families, where children are raised without fathers. This concern has been expressed in policies supported by all political parties aimed at reducing state expenditure and, particularly, the costs of supporting 'single'-mother families through social security benefits. Additional concerns focus around the costs of divorce proceedings and of resolving disputes over children and other ancillary matters through the courts. This chapter looks at legislation enacted over the last decade which reflects these concerns and discusses its impact on lesbian parenting.

THE CHILDREN ACT 1989

Parental responsibility

The Children Act has been heralded as a progressive piece of legislation, ostensibly focusing more on the needs and wishes of children and making it easier for non-biological carers to gain legal recognition of their parenting role. This latter aspect of the Act has particularly benefited lesbian parents. It must not be forgotten, however, that one of the main purposes of the Act was to redress the balance where it was felt that the non-custodial parent (usually the father) had lost his rights to make decisions about children after divorce or separation. It was felt that sole custody orders put women 'in the driving seat' in relation to children,[1] typically by giving them the opportunity to deliberately block men's access to children. For several years prior to the implementation of the Act fathers' rights groups, such as Families Need Fathers, had been lobbying for joint custody on divorce as well as automatic rights to children for unmarried fathers.[2]

The Act introduced a whole new language to define parents' relationships to their children, doing away with language such as custody and introducing the concept of parental responsibility, which for married parents would continue after divorce. This concept was ostensibly intended to move the emphasis away from parental rights and to stress the responsibilities involved in the parental relationship. However, the definition of parental responsibility in the Act still retains the notion of parental rights and authority:

In this act 'parental responsibility' means all the rights, duties, powers, responsibilities and authority which by law a parent has in relation to the child and his (sic) property. (Children Act 1989 s. 3)

The Act did not give unmarried fathers automatic rights in relation to children. Unmarried women retain sole parental responsibility. It did, however, make it possible for unmarried fathers to apply for parental responsibility through the courts or by making a legal agreement with the mother. No party other than an unmarried father has the right to make a free-standing application for, or agreement to, parental responsibility.

The Act also introduced another innovation by allowing each party with parental responsibility to take independent decisions regarding a child when the child is with her or him, providing this does not contravene a court order. Most frequently, this would involve decisions on, for example, medical treatment and education. This has had contradictory implications for lesbian parents, as is discussed below.

Court orders

Residence and contact
In conjunction with the concept of continuing parental responsibility the Children Act also changed the language and the types of orders for which disputing carers may apply (s. 8 (1)). A residence order replaces the old concept of 'care and control' and states with whom a child should live. It automatically confers parental responsibility.

The Act allows for the possibility of joint residence orders, and it was envisaged that these orders would be used as an alternative to one parent having a sole residence order, thus again stressing a father's right to continuing involvement with children on divorce or separation. The replacement of the term 'access' with 'contact' orders emphasises that contact with the non-residential parent is the right of the child.

The Act also introduced the possibility of children being able to apply for such orders on their own behalf, if they obtained leave of the court and could demonstrate sufficient understanding to make the application (s. 10 (8)). However, caselaw has demonstrated that in general the courts do not look favourably on children making such applications.

Prohibited steps and specific issue orders

The Act allows parties with parental responsibility to make some decisions independently of each other when the child is with them, and it also introduced two new orders for which either parent could apply if they wished to stop the other taking certain actions. A prohibited steps order prevents a parent from taking a specific action, such as removing a child to live abroad, or from changing a child's school. A specific issue order deals with a particular issue concerned with a child's upbringing such as where she should go to school or her health care.

The welfare principle

The Act also introduced a welfare checklist to guide the courts in interpreting what is in the best interests of the children in disputes between parents. In general this checklist incorporated previous guiding principles, developed by precedent, for dealing with parental disputes, although with a renewed emphasis on the wishes of the children. In addition, it introduced the concept of not making an order at all if it was felt this was in the best interests of the child. This non-interventionist principle is based on the assumption that court battles can aggravate conflict between parents, which will then impinge on the child. It also assumes that most parents will behave reasonably in working out arrangements for the children without resorting to the law. It thus anticipated moves towards the informal resolving of disputes through mediation introduced by the Family Law Act 1996, which is discussed later in this chapter.

The Children Act also extended the inherent jurisdiction of a court to make orders where none had been applied for, for example a contact order, if the court believed it was in the best interests of the child (s. 10 (1) (b)).

Consequences for lesbian parents

The impact of the Children Act for lesbian parents has been contradictory. One of the main consequences has been that the courts have interpreted the idea of continuing parental responsibility on divorce as meaning that fathers should, in the vast majority of cases, have reasonable ongoing contact with the children when they live with their mother.

This legal presumption has codified the prevailing tendency to override other considerations such as the father's capability to meet a child's needs or risk of harm to the child, both of which are now within the welfare checklist. In particular, courts have tended to discount domestic violence and its impact on the child and/or mother as a reason why a father should not have contact.

Research in this area has demonstrated that a father who merely expresses a wish to see the children is seen as 'a good enough father' by court welfare officers and judges, and thus contact is granted. Additionally, research has suggested that where children express a wish for no contact with a father, or where a child's views are ambiguous, these are ignored by court welfare officers and judges.[3]

Lesbian mothers who keep residence of their children on divorce are therefore expected to agree to reasonable contact arrangements with the father, whatever his ability to care for the children or his conduct towards the mother. In our previous and current research on lesbian mothers' experiences of contact arrangements this has often been used by fathers as a means to continue to harass and abuse the mother physically and/or verbally, and to undermine her parenting role.

On the other hand, lesbian mothers who have been married and who themselves give up living with the children, or where the father gains a residence order, are also usually expected to have reasonable contact. In some cases, however, lesbian mothers may still have their contact arrangements scrutinised by the courts, particularly where they are living with a lesbian partner.

The right of each party with parental responsibility to take independent action, and the consequences of prohibited steps orders, can also have contradictory implications for lesbian mothers who retain residence of their children. Fathers have used prohibited steps orders to continue to interfere in a mother's upbringing of children, for example, by preventing a mother moving a child to a different school nearer to where she lives. On the other hand, mothers have also been able to use such orders where they fear a father might abduct the children, or to prevent him harming the children on contact visits.

Lesbian mothers who have sole parental responsibility, either because they were not married to the biological father or have a child born through self-insemination where the donor is known, can also face the father making an application to court for a contact order. Whilst it is possible for a mother to oppose such an order, it is unusual for the courts to refuse contact, because of the legal presumptions discussed above. This may be the case even where a father has had little or no contact with the child in the past.

THE FAMILY LAW ACT 1996

The Family Law Act introduces a number of new provisions. These affect the way a divorce can be obtained, the means of resolving disputes over children and other matters, and protection for women from domestic violence. These changes come into effect in two stages, with the provisions on domestic violence being implemented first in October 1997, and new means of obtaining a divorce and dispute resolution being implemented in January 1999.

Divorce

The divorce provisions found in the Act reflect the state's concerns with the huge increase in the divorce rate over the previous two and a half decades since the liberalisation of divorce in 1969. One of the major ideological concerns, particularly from the traditional right and 'family values' lobby, has been women's 'flight' from marriage and a fear that living outside of marriage has become 'too attractive to women.'[4]

The majority of divorce applications are made by women (71 per cent in 1994, according to Office of Population Censuses and Surveys statistics), and three-fifths of divorce applications also involve dependent children. A divorce can also currently be obtained within six or seven months where grounds such as unreasonable behaviour or adultery are used. Far fewer women remarry than men, and many now choose to live as 'single' parents.[5]

The Act makes it harder for women with children to leave marriages by lengthening the minimum time it takes to get divorced. It also requires divorce applicants to negotiate a series of obstacles, which includes agreeing with the other partner on financial and property matters as well as arrangements for the children, before a divorce order can be obtained. Whilst one of the much-publicised clauses of the Act does away with having to cite grounds for the divorce, this in itself does not affect the length of time or the difficulties involved in obtaining a divorce in the future.

One of the stated aims of the legislation is 'to encourage [the parties] whether by marriage counselling or otherwise to save the marriage' (Family Law Act 1996, s. 1(b)). For this purpose it introduces 'a period of reflection and consideration'. For people with children this means that there is a minimum wait of eighteen months after taking the first steps to initiate a divorce, before it will be granted. To begin the divorce process, the person initiating the divorce must first attend an information session, where they will be given information about marriage guidance counselling and be told about the importance of considering the welfare of the children.

The Act also underlines the presumption of ongoing paternal contact, brought about by the Children Act 1989, stating that where a divorce order is made the welfare of the child will best be served by 'his [sic] having regular contact with those who have parental responsibility for him and with other members of his family' (s. 11 (4) (c)).

Mediated agreements

An implicit purpose of the Act is to save the state money, particularly in relation to the legal aid costs of obtaining a divorce. Again, it is women who will be largely disadvantaged by these measures, as five out of six women currently receive legal aid to obtain a divorce and resolve 'ancillary matters' such as the arrangements for the children, finance and property matters.[6]

In order to save on legal costs and court hearings the Act proposes that disputes between the divorcing parties should generally be resolved through mediated agreements. Legal aid, for those who qualify, will be paid for mediation rather than for legal advice and representation, except in certain circumstances where mediation is regarded as unsuitable, such as where there has been domestic violence.

Research from abroad and in this country suggests that mediation disadvantages women in the divorce process, particularly in the division of any financial assets and arrangements for the children, since there is no one to represent and protect their interests.[7] Mediation is based on the premise that women and men enter the process on a basis of equality. It ignores the power imbalances that exist between them and that are supported by wider structural inequalities, including economic ones, where women may be earning far less than men, or, if they are caring for children full-time, may have no sources of income of their own. Mediation supposedly empowers the parties to come to their own decisions, yet where power imbalances already exist, women are unlikely to feel empowered, especially where they are put into a situation where they are being pressurised by the expectations of the mediator, as well as being intimidated by a more powerful male partner. Mediators do not themselves start with unbiased assumptions, and these have been shown to influence the outcomes of mediation.[8]

Sexuality, ethnicity and class

Other considerations also arise, including who will be commissioned to act as mediators and what training mediators will receive. Most of the mediation that has been undertaken in this country has been carried out, so far, by white, middle-class women. There is no provision within the Act to take account of the needs of ethnic minorities or to consider, for example, language needs. As far as lesbian parents are concerned it is unlikely that mediators will have received training in heterosexism awareness or will necessarily come to the mediation process with unprejudiced attitudes towards lesbian mothers. Further, most mediators do not have any legal training, and any mediated agreements between the parties will still need to be checked by a solicitor. It is not yet clear whether legal aid will be available for this.

Mediation for family disputes outside of divorce
The Act also amends the Legal Aid Act 1988 to provide for all disputes involving family matters, including residence or contact issues around children, to be resolved through mediation (Part III, amending s. 13 (a) of the Legal Aid Act 1988). This means that even where the partners in dispute have never been married, it is still expected that they will enter mediation rather than resolve the dispute by having legal representation and/or going to the courts. This will also affect disputes between lesbian parents.

Divorce and the welfare of the children
An explicit principle of the Act and in particular the move towards mediated agreements is to enable the parties to resolve disputes amicably, 'with the minimum of distress to the parties and the children affected' (s. 1 (c)). While this is a laudable aim, it fails to take account of the realities of marriage breakdown and the bitterness and acrimony that often accompany it. Lesbian mothers frequently experience intense hostility from male partners when the marriage is ending because of a mother's lesbianism. Current arrange-ments for in-court mediation (also known as conciliation) often fail to resolve residence disputes in these circumstances, because such hostility exists.

The domestic violence provisions

These provisions came about as a result of intense feminist campaigning to provide greater protection for women experiencing domestic violence. They make it easier for a woman to obtain a court order (injunction) to protect her own safety and that of her children, and also to allow her to stay in the matrimonial home. Domestic violence is also recognised in the divorce provisions of the Act, enabling a woman who has such court orders to obtain a divorce within 12 months, rather than having to wait the statutory 18 months. However, ss. 36, 38 and 41 of the Act clearly discriminate between women who have been cohabiting with a male partner and those who are/have been married, making it harder in some situations for former cohabitants to obtain protection.

Lesbian mothers who are experiencing domestic violence from male partners will be able to take advantage of these provisions, particularly where they wish to speed up the divorce process. But the Act does not address the issue of violent fathers having contact with children and so fails to offer protection to the large numbers of women who continue to experience violence from ex-partners during contact hand-over times.

The domestic violence provisions also enable a lesbian parent who is experiencing violence from a lesbian partner to take out a court order in certain circumstances. (See also Chapter Seven and Chapter Eleven.)

THE CHILD SUPPORT ACT 1991

The Child Support Act 1991 is concerned with issues of child maintenance, but its implications are far wider than this, since it presupposes that mothers should be dependent on individual men for their own maintenance as well as the financial support of their children, rather than on the state. Accessibility to state benefits for 'single' mothers in the past has enabled them to gain a relative autonomy, albeit on a

very low income, from male control within the family. The
implications of the Child Support Act are that such autonomy
is no longer possible, unless a mother is able to support
herself and her children through her own earnings.

One of the purposes of the Act was to reduce state costs
of supporting 'single' mothers on benefits by making all biological or adoptive fathers responsible for child maintenance
and the maintenance of mothers themselves. The Act pays no
regard to marital status, or to a father's relationship to the
children, or to whether the mother wishes to claim maintenance from him. It requires any 'absent' parent (defined as
someone who does not live in the same household) to pay
child support to 'the person with care'. Women who are
on benefits and claiming income support, family credit or
disability working allowance are required to cooperate with
the Child Support Agency (CSA) in providing it with information that would enable it to pursue the absent father for
child support. Where they refuse to cooperate with the CSA
they are likely to have their benefit penalised, unless they can
show good cause.

The implications for lesbian parents

For lesbian mothers who are leaving or intending to leave a
heterosexual relationship and have no income of their own,
the Act can make it much harder to be able to negotiate any
agreement about where the children should live on separation. The fact that a father has to pay child support can
increase his opposition to agreeing that the children should
live with their mother. Lesbian mothers who do not have
their children living with them are also required to pay child
support if the father is claiming the benefits described above.

For lesbian mothers who have had their children through
a casual sexual encounter or self-insemination with a known
donor, the Act also creates problems, as the CSA will still
regard him as the biological father, irrespective of any
relationship to the child or prior agreement made with the
mother. However, individual CSA officers have limited discre-

tion to accept 'good cause'. This is discussed further in Chapter Nine.

The Act does not apply where women are able to support children through their own income, as it is at their discretion whether they choose to claim child support or not.

NOTES

1. A Bainham, *Children and the New Law: The Children Act 1989*, Family Law, London, 1990.

2. Julia Brophy, 'Custody Law: Childcare and Inequality' in C Smart and S Sevenhuijsen, eds, *Child Custody and the Politics of Gender*, Routledge, London, 1989; Lynne Harne and Jill Radford, 'The Politics of the Family and the New Legislation' in Audrey Mullender and Rebecca Morley, eds, *Children Living with Domestic Violence: Putting Men's Abuse of Women on the Childcare Agenda*, Whiting and Birch, London, 1994.

3. Marianne Hester and Lorraine Radford, *Domestic Violence and Child Contact Arrangements in England and Denmark*, Policy Press, Bristol, 1996.

4. Hilary Land, 'Families and the Law' in John Muncie et al, eds, *Understanding the Family*, Sage, London, 1995, p93.

5. See Hilary Land, 'Families and the Law'.

6. See Hilary Land, 'Families and the Law'.

7. Lorraine Radford, 'Domestic Violence, Child Contact and Mediation', *Rights of Women Bulletin* (Autumn 1994); Shelley Day Sclater, 'Divorce Law Changes – The Psychology of Dispute Resolution', *Rights of Women Bulletin* (Summer 1995).

8. Shelley Day Sclater, 'Divorce Law Changes – The Psychology of Dispute Resolution'.

CHAPTER 3

LESBIAN MOTHERS – BETTER PARENTS?

Psychological evidence on children and parental relationships in lesbian households

Psychological research on children growing up in lesbian households began in the mid-1970s and is continuing today. Early research aimed to challenge the prejudiced assumptions of the courts and has largely been successful in doing so, whilst more recent studies have found particular advantages for children growing up in such environments, with particular reference to children growing up in lesbian households from birth. The psychological evidence cited here is used not as a defensive argument but to provide background information which has been proved relevant in winning residence cases, and more recently in supporting arguments for lesbians having access to donor insemination, as well as being able to foster and adopt.

THE PSYCHOLOGICAL STANDPOINT

Much of the psychological research on children in lesbian families has been, and still is, conducted from a normative standpoint. A central assumption is that it is preferable for children to grow up to be heterosexual rather than lesbian or gay. Some research also assumes that it is better for children to conform to the gender stereotypes (ie ideas about masculinity and femininity) that still prevail in much of Western society. This approach has had advantages in enabling lesbian mothers to gain residence of their children in legal disputes and in supporting arguments for lesbians being able to foster and adopt. However, much of it also creates dilemmas for those people who may wish to challenge such values and assumptions. More recently some research on lesbian households has begun to challenge such normative values, and these studies, as well as the views of children themselves, are discussed in the latter half of this chapter.

THE COURTS' CONCERNS

Lesbians' parenting abilities

Some of the earliest concerns of the courts in the 1970s centred on lesbians' parenting abilities. Lesbians were seen only in terms of their sexuality, which itself was attributed to the result of faulty personality development. Lesbian mothers were believed to be 'emotionally unstable and prone to psychiatric disorder . . . not maternal, and (it was thought) that they or their partner might sexually abuse the children'.[1]

These assumptions appeared to be based on the belief that lesbians are over-sexed and that they adopt the worst aspects of masculine sexual behaviour. It was thought that, since it was unimaginable that women could have an independent sexual identity of their own, lesbians must imitate male sexuality in its most predatory manifestations. Further, the conclusions drawn regarding a supposed lack of maternal feeling in lesbians was based on the notion that lesbians would put their own sexual needs before care for their children.

The psychosexual development of children

What psychologists call psychosexual development and identity may be defined as follows:

sexual orientation or object choice – whether a person

chooses to have heterosexual or lesbian or gay sexual relationships

gender identity – people's concept of themselves as female or male

gender-role behaviour – those behavioural features which have been designated by society as most appropriate to females or males[2]

Sexual orientation

One of the courts' main concerns has been that children living in lesbian households would themselves grow up to be lesbian or gay. In the early days the courts described this as the possibility of 'corruption'. It was thought that mothers either directly or 'by force of example' would be able to persuade their children to become lesbian or gay and resist all the social forces which assume that being heterosexual is the most desirable way to be. It can be cogently argued that lesbian mothers are able to present a choice about sexuality to their children which can be seen as a positive benefit.

Gender-role behaviour

Another issue raised was that children would be influenced by their lesbian mothers to step out of the prescribed gender roles that children of both sexes are still expected to adopt in our society including, for example, the expectation that children should show an interest in 'appropriate' toys, guns for boys and dolls for girls. That such gender-role behaviour might not be desirable for either girls or boys was not questioned.

Some lesbian mothers fear that if they have sons, they will have less chance of obtaining a residence order. Although this was true in the seventies and early eighties, it is less of a concern now. Research on lesbian mothers bringing up boys has shown that boys receive male influences largely from their own peer group and from other factors such as television or maternal male relatives. In most cases they will also continue to have contact with their fathers.

Gender identity

A third concern was in the area of gender identity itself, the question of whether a person sees herself/himself as female or male. It was thought that in growing up with lesbian mothers children might be confused about their own gender identity. This particular belief stemmed from the Freudian suggestion that young children need both a mother and a father in order to be confirmed in their own gender identity. Such a theory has never been supported by empirical evidence, as demonstrated by the enormous number of children who have grown up in women-headed families.

Social stigma

Another main area with which the courts were concerned was that children of lesbian mothers might experience social stigma, particularly from their peers. In the early days this was described as the effect of 'reputation'. Such an argument was circular, since by making such an assumption the courts were themselves reinforcing social prejudice. Further, the logic of such an argument was that any child growing up in any family which did not fit the white, two-parent family norm ran the risk of removal from home because they were likely to experience prejudice and discrimination.

Children's mental and emotional well-being

A final concern was that children's mental and emotional well-being in general might be affected as a result of growing up in a woman-only or lesbian household. This need not relate specifically to children growing up in lesbian households and has developed from psychological assumptions that 'some childhood family experiences carry an increased risk of childhood disorder'.[3] It is not clear why such fears should be aimed specifically at lesbian households, except that they are regarded as non-traditional, and indeed similar assumptions are made about all children in women-headed families, whatever the sexual orientation of the mother.

It is largely the concerns around psychosexual development, the social stigma suffered by children, and their mental and emotional well-being that have remained the focus of residence disputes involving lesbian mothers over the last few years.

THE PSYCHOLOGICAL RESEARCH FINDINGS

Much of the research that has been carried out on lesbian parenting has been undertaken in the US. Some major research has taken place in Britain,[4] however, and this has been extremely influential in affecting court decisions concerning lesbian mothers in Britain. A study following up on that research has also been undertaken on the same children who are now young adults.[5] This study confirms the earlier findings and highlights some of the benefits enjoyed by children growing up in lesbian households. The majority of the research undertaken compares children from lesbian households with children from single-heterosexual-mother households in order to allow a control sample for the 'lesbian factor'. Lone heterosexual mothers tend to be regarded as women who are not living with a male partner at the time of the research. Many of the research findings are also placed in the context of established population norms where these are available.

Lesbians' parenting abilities

The myth that lesbian mothers are more likely to suffer from psychiatric disorders was one of the first to be dispelled by psychological research.[6] Contrary to such prejudiced beliefs, many of these studies found that lesbians are more self-confident, less neurotic and more independent and self-sufficient than their heterosexual counterparts.

Nor did the research findings demonstrate that lesbian mothers were less child-centred, nurturant and responsive to their children than heterosexual women.[7] The daily life of lesbian mothers has been shown to be as centred around their children as that of heterosexual mothers.[8]

The myth that lesbian mothers are likely to sexually abuse their children has been dispelled by research into the incidence of child abuse, which has found that the vast majority of sexual abuse of children is carried out by men.[9]

Research into children's psychosexual development

The earlier British study, entitled 'Children in Lesbian and Single-Parent Households: Psychosexual and Psychiatric Appraisal',[10] has been cited as one of the most authoritative pieces of research into the area and confirmed a number of American studies that had already been undertaken. The study compared 37 school-age children in lesbian households with 38 school-age children in heterosexual households which are headed by women following divorce or separation. The focus of the research was the three areas of psychosexual development defined earlier: gender identity, sexual orientation and gender-role behaviour.

Gender identity
The British study found no children in either group had problems with their gender identity. A more recent study on 37 children born mainly through artificial insemination showed that children of lesbian mothers have no difficulty with the establishment of gender identity.[11] In 1992 the same researcher confirmed that no children of lesbians already researched, estimated at more than 300, have shown any evidence of gender confusion.[12]

Sexual orientation
In the initial British study,[13] 11 adolescent children were studied and it was found that these children showed a typical pattern of development, reporting mostly heterosexual

crushes. No difference emerged according to family type. This result was replicated several years later by an American study which compared the sexual orientation of 18 children aged 13–19 years of both lesbian and heterosexual mothers.[14] Another American study, comparing the sexual orientation of adult daughters of both lesbian and heterosexual mothers, found that their sexual orientation was not related to their parents' sexuality and was normative compared with the general population.[15]

The British follow-up study,[16] in which 46 young adults from the original cohort were interviewed again, found no significant difference in sexual orientation between the two groups. However, the study's findings were that 'young adults from lesbian family backgrounds were significantly more likely to report having considered the possibility of becoming involved in a same-gender relationship' than those from the heterosexual family control group. The researchers suggest that this difference may be due to the fact that young adults from the heterosexual family group appeared to be less comfortable in talking about lesbian and gay issues generally, and that having a lesbian mother appeared to widen young adults' views of 'what constituted acceptable sexual behaviour to include same-gender sexual relationships'.[17]

Gender-role behaviour

The earlier British study[18] found that there were no differences between lesbian and heterosexual families in terms of children's gender-role behaviour. This conclusion replicated those found by earlier American studies.[19] In fact, the British study investigating children's preferred toys, games, activities and friendships found that children from both groups displayed 'rather traditional behaviour'.

Research into children's experience of social relationships

This research has looked specifically at the courts' assumption that children of lesbians will have their social relationships impaired as a result of experiencing social stigma from their peers. Assumptions have been made that children will be teased and ostracised as a consequence of their mother's identity and that this in itself will affect their ability to form and maintain friendships with other children.

The earlier British study[20] looked at children's social relationships with their peers through interviews with their mothers. It found that there was no difference in the reported quality of children's social relationships between the children of lesbian-mother households and those of lone-parent, heterosexual-mother households. A US study, which looked at both children's and mothers' perceptions of childhood peer-group relationships, also found no significant difference between lesbian-mother or lone-parent, heterosexual-mother families.[21]

The British follow-up study[22] directly asked young adults who had been part of the earlier study specific questions about memories of their peer-group relationships as children. They were questioned as to whether they remembered being teased or bullied about their own sexuality and/or that of their mother, whether their friends knew about their mother's sexual orientation, and responses of friends who knew. It again found no significant difference between incidences of teasing or bullying between the two groups. Most of the 23 young adults with lesbian mothers had felt able to control access to information about their mother's sexual orientation amongst their friends, and 14 had felt able to tell at least one close friend. The majority had not met with hostile responses from friends they did inform.

These findings indicate that courts' concerns about the effect of a mother's lesbian identity on their children's peer-group relationships are unfounded.

Research into children's well-being

The 1983 British study looked explicitly at children's emotional development and behaviour. Methodology included questionnaires for teachers and interviews with parents and their children. The study found 'no statistically

significant differences between children of lesbian or heterosexual mothers', and any incidence of disorder was 'similar
to that found for children in heterosexual two-parent families'.[23] The follow-up study,[24] which tested participants for
anxiety and depression, also found that there was no significant difference between the two cohorts of young adults, and
the scores for both groups matched those amongst the wider
population for the age group.

A US study looking at personality characteristics among
adult daughters of lesbian and heterosexual mothers found
that there was no significant difference between the two
groups, except on the scale called 'well being', where adult
daughters of lesbians scored more favourably than daughters
of heterosexual mothers.[25]

This research evidence challenges the assumptions and fears
of courts about the effects of children growing up in lesbian
households.

BENEFITS OF CHILDREN GROWING UP IN LESBIAN HOUSEHOLDS

The above research studies show that in many areas there
are no significant differences between children being brought
up by lesbians and those being brought up by lone-parent,
heterosexual mothers. This is not a surprising result given
the now widely accepted view that children's development
is greatly influenced by the social environment beyond the
family.

Some research has also begun to highlight the positive
aspects of being brought up by lesbian parents. The British
follow-up study found that young adults in lesbian households 'described their relationship with their mother's partner
significantly more positively than those who had been raised
by a heterosexual mother and a new male partner.' Young
adults from lesbian households 'were more likely to be proud
of their mother's sexual identity', which they saw as 'a
political matter' through which they sought to influence
public opinion.[26]

Similar benefits have also been highlighted by exploratory

research into lesbian families. In one study children of lesbian mothers reported an increased tolerance for divergent viewpoints as one benefit of growing up in a lesbian household.[27] This accords with ROW's own interviews with lesbian mothers who have had children through donor insemination, extracts of which appear in Chapter Eight.

A study of 37 lesbian households, involving pre-school and school-aged children predominantly born through donor insemination, found that these children reported more positive emotional feelings, for example joy and contentment, than children living in heterosexual households.[28] A study of gender-role behaviour of lesbian parents' children found that there was less sex-stereotyped preference for school and social activities than among children of lone heterosexual mothers.[29]

Two small clinical studies conducted in the 1980s found that children may benefit from their mother living with a lesbian partner.[30] However, because of the small size of these samples any conclusions need to be treated with caution. Variations may well depend on the kind of relationship a partner has with the child and the age of the children involved. Children who have grown up from an early age with two mothers often describe benefits of this type of household.[31]

RESEARCH ON EFFECTS ON CHILDREN OF KNOWING THEIR MOTHER IS A LESBIAN

One study suggests that a mother's openness with her child, and the extent to which she understands any difficulties which the child may have, for example in presenting their home situation to friends at school, can benefit both the mother-child relationship and the child's well-being in general.[32] This study suggests that children who find out about their mother's lesbianism by accident, or are told for some other reason, may find it more difficult to accept. These results also need to be compared with samples of children growing up in heterosexual families where they accidentally discover that their mother has begun a new relationship.

Another study found that children who learnt of their mothers' lesbianism in childhood had higher self-esteem than those who were not informed of her sexual orientation until their early adolescence.[33] It further found that children whose fathers rejected their mother's lesbianism reported lower self-esteem than those whose fathers were neutral or positive. Whilst these theories are far from conclusive due to the small sample size, they do suggest that openness and acceptance of the mother's lesbianism by close adult role models impinge on a child's well-being.

EVIDENCE FROM CHILDREN THEMSELVES

A US book, *Different Mothers*, reports 38 experiences of children of different ages growing up in a variety of lesbian households.[34] The study includes children from differing races and backgrounds. Whilst the vast majority of children had grown up in lesbian households after their parents had divorced, a very few were children by donor insemination or children who had been adopted. The vast majority of these children described how important it was to them to know their mother was a lesbian, and to be able to understand and discuss it, even though it was something they might need to handle discreetly at school. The findings discussed below are from this book.

Two mothers

Those children who had grown up with two mothers from a young age described this as positive, with one child saying her friends were 'jealous of her having two mums'. Children who had developed a relationship with a non-biological mother, or with their mother's partner, described how important it was for them to continue with this, even when the mother and her partner had separated. For older children, individual variations were reported on how well they related to their mother's lover, seemingly depending on the individual personalities involved.

Attitudes of fathers and others

A number of children who had contact with their fathers or other relatives such as grandparents described how painful it was for them if these relatives expressed negative attitudes towards lesbians. Where fathers do express hostility towards the mother's sexual orientation, this may be a factor which is regarded in a negative light by the courts (see the case of *C v C* 1991, discussed in Chapter Four).

School and friends

Children's experiences in this area differed and, as could be expected, younger children had fewer problems with attitudes at school, either from their peer group or teachers. Older children often said they kept quiet about their mothers being lesbian because of anti-gay prejudice from both teachers and peers The vast majority of children reported that they had not been unduly affected, however, and they all recognised that the problem rested in discriminatory social attitudes rather than with their mothers.

Many children described how growing up in a lesbian household and/or lesbian communities had enriched their lives. Some talked about the importance of knowing other children of lesbian mothers, and others also talked about the importance of having adult friends who were lesbian or gay.

CONCLUSION

Whilst the myths about children living in lesbian families have largely been dispelled by psychological research, the many benefits for children growing up in such households still need to be developed in research programmes. The assumption that lesbian households are second best to a two-parent, heterosexual family still prevails in much research, as does the view that discrimination and prejudiced attitudes in social institutions such as schools are inevitable rather than something to be challenged within these institutions themselves.

NOTES

1. Fiona Tasker and Susan Golombok, 'Adults Raised as Children in Lesbian Families', *American Journal of Orthopsychiatry* 65, 2 (April 1995), p205.

2. Michael Rutter, 'Psychosexual Development' in Michael Rutter, ed, *Scientific Foundations of Development Psychiatry*, Heinemann Medical, London, 1980.

3. Fiona Tasker and Susan Golombok, 'Children Raised by Lesbian Mothers: The Empirical Evidence', *Fam Law* 21 (1991), pp184–7.

4. Susan Golombok, Ann Spencer and Michael Rutter, 'Children in Lesbian and Single-Parent Households: Psychosexual and Psychiatric Appraisal', *Journal of Child Psychology and Psychiatry* 124, 4 (1983), pp551–72.

5. Fiona Tasker and Susan Golombok, 'Adults Raised as Children in Lesbian Families'.

6. DJ West, ed, *Homosexuality Reexamined*, Duckworth, London, 1977; AP Bell and MS Weinberg, *Homosexualities: A Study of Diversity Among Men and Women*, Simon & Schuster, New York, 1978.

7. BM Mucklow and GK Phelan, 'Lesbian and Traditional Mothers' Responses to Child Behavior and Self-concept', *Psychological Reports* 44 (1979), pp880–2; JA Miller, et al, 'The Child's Home Environment for Lesbian vs Heterosexual Mothers: A Neglected Area of Research', *Journal of Homosexuality* 7 (1981) pp49–56; Susan Golombok, Ann Spencer and Michael Rutter, 'Children in Lesbian and Single-Parent Households: Psychosexual and Psychiatric Appraisal'.

8. MD Pagelow, 'Heterosexual and Lesbian Single Mothers: A Comparison of Problems, Coping and Solutions', *Journal of Homosexuality* 5 (1980), pp198–204; Martha Kirkpatrick, 'Clinical Implications of Lesbian Mother Studies', *Journal of Homosexuality* 13 (1987), pp201–11.

9. D Finkelor and D Russell, 'Women as Perpetrators' in D Finkelor, ed, *Child Sexual Abuse: New Theory and Research*, Free Press, New York, 1984.

10. Susan Golombok, Ann Spencer and Michael Rutter, 'Children in Lesbian and Single-Parent Households: Psychosexual and Psychiatric Appraisal'.

11. Charlotte Patterson, 'Children of the Lesbian Baby Boom' in Beverly Greene and Gregory M Herek, eds, *Contemporary Perspectives on Gay and Lesbian Psychology: Theory, Research and Applications*, Sage, Beverly Hills, California, 1991.

12. Charlotte Patterson, 'Children of Lesbian and Gay Parents', *Child Development* 63 (1992), pp1025–42.

13. Susan Golombok, Ann Spencer and Michael Rutter, 'Children in Lesbian and Single-Parent Households: Psychosexual and Psychiatric Appraisal'.

14. SL Huggins, 'A Comparative Study of Self-Esteem of Adolescent Children of Divorced Lesbian Mothers and Divorced Heterosexual Mothers' in FW Bozett, ed, *Homosexuality and the Family*, Harrington Park Press, New York, 1989.

15. JS Gottman, 'Children of Gay and Lesbian Parents' in FW Bozett and MB Sussman, eds, *Homosexuality and Family Relations*, Harrington Park Press, New York, 1990.

16. Fiona Tasker and Susan Golombok, 'Adults Raised as Children in Lesbian Families'.

17. Fiona Tasker and Susan Golombok, 'Adults Raised as Children in Lesbian Families', pp210, 212–13.

18. Susan Golombok, Ann Spencer and Michael Rutter, 'Children in Lesbian and Single-Parent Households: Psychosexual and Psychiatric Appraisal'.

19. Richard Green, 'Sexual Identity of 37 Children Raised by Homosexual or Transsexual Parents', *American Journal of Psychiatry* 135 (1978) pp692–7; Martha Kirkpatrick, et al, 'Lesbian Mothers and Their Children: A Comparative Study', *American Journal of Orthopsychiatry* 51 (1981), pp545–51; B Hoeffer, 'Children's Acquisition of Sex-Role Behavior in Lesbian-Mother Families', *American Journal of Orthopsychiatry* 5 (1981), pp536–44.

20. Susan Golombok, Ann Spencer and Michael Rutter, 'Children in Lesbian and Single-Parent Households: Psychosexual and Psychiatric Appraisal'.

21. Richard Green, et al, 'Lesbian Mothers and their Children: A Comparison with Solo Parent Heterosexual Mothers and their Children', *Archives of Sexual Behavior* 15, 2 (1986), pp166–84.

22. Fiona Tasker and Susan Golombok, 'Adults Raised as Children in Lesbian Families'.

23. Fiona Tasker and Susan Golombok, 'Children Raised by Lesbian Mothers: The Empirical Evidence'.

24. Fiona Tasker and Susan Golombok, 'Adults Raised as Children in Lesbian Families'.

25. JS Gottman, 'Children of Gay and Lesbian Parents'.

26. Fiona Tasker and Susan Golombok, 'Adults Raised as Children in Lesbian Families', p209.

27. L Rafkin, ed, *Different Mothers: Sons and Daughters of Lesbians Talk about their Lives*, Cleis Press, Pittsburgh, 1990.

28. Charlotte Patterson, 'Children of the Lesbian Baby Boom'.

29. Richard Green, et al, 'Lesbian Mothers and their Children: A Comparison with Solo Parent Heterosexual Mothers and their Children'.

30. SL Huggins, 'A Comparative Study of Self-Esteem of Adolescent Children of Divorced Lesbian Mothers and Divorced Heterosexual Mothers'; Martha Kirkpatrick, 'Clinical Implications of Lesbian Mother Studies'.

31. L Rafkin, ed, *Different Mothers*.

32. S Pennington, 'Children of Lesbian Mothers' in FW Bozett, ed, *Gay and Lesbian Parents*, Praeger, New York, 1987.

33. SL Huggins, 'A Comparative Study of Self-Esteem of Adolescent Children of Divorced Lesbian Mothers and Divorced Heterosexual Mothers'.

34. L Rafkin, ed, *Different Mothers*.

CHAPTER 4

VALUABLE JUDGMENTS

Recent court cases

During the late seventies and early eighties there were a number of reported cases involving lesbian mothers. Many of the judgments in these cases revealed high levels of prejudice against lesbians. Over recent years this level of prejudice has begun to subside and in some courts may be totally absent. In part this is due to the increasing amount of research undertaken into children growing up in lesbian households, as described in Chapter Three.

ROW's experience indicates that High Court judges are currently taking a more pragmatic view of lesbian parenting, although provincial county courts may still demonstrate ignorance and prejudice. The Court of Appeal has continued to be problematic for lesbian mothers. But in most recent cases the Appeal Court has been reluctant to overturn judgments made below them and thus has moved a long way in the past twenty years.

This chapter gives an overview of the few reported cases and appeal judgments that have been made since the beginning of the 1990s, as these are now the most relevant for lesbian mothers and legal advisors involved in residence applications or disputes.

Since 1990, there have been only two reported cases involving disputes between a lesbian mother and a father over residence of children. A third reported case involves an application by two lesbians for a residence order of a child they proposed to adopt. Both the reported cases involving residence disputes were heard prior to the Children Act 1989 coming into operation. They therefore use the old terms, 'custody' and 'care and control' (residence), in the reporting of the legal judgments. In both these cases the mother was awarded care and control of the child in question, and consequently they form important precedents for women in similar positions. Both cases were heard in the Family Division of the High Court, and the second case then went to appeal.

B v B[1]

The dispute involved the youngest child of a family, a boy then aged two. By the parents' mutual agreement the two older children were to live with their father. The judgment in this case is significant because it went against the recommendations of the court welfare officer (CWO) due to the use of expert evidence by the mother's legal team.

In 1988 the mother left the matrimonial home to have a relationship with another woman. The youngest son, then aged seven months, remained with her. At the time of the hearing in 1990, the mother was living with her lover in a two-bedroomed cottage. The father was living with the two eldest children in a four-bedroomed house. He had started a new relationship with another woman whom he hoped to marry later in the year. The two older children – aged ten and nine years, a girl and a boy – had been living with the father for most of the time since the mother left and had expressed a wish to remain with him. There had originally been cross-applications for custody of all three children, but the mother had later agreed that the oldest children should live with the father, since this was what they wanted.

The welfare report recommended that the youngest child (who was by then aged two) should live with the father for three reasons: concern about the effect of the mother's lesbianism on the child; concern that if the father lost care and control he would make a fresh application when the boy was older; and the belief that siblings should remain together.

On examination of the first reason given, His Honour Judge Callman, sitting as a High Court judge, outlined two main concerns: the effect on the psychosexual development of the child and the fear that the child would be taunted or ostracised. In reaching his decision that the mother should have care and control of the child the judge said:

> In this case I have had the inestimable advantage of having had an eminent expert in the person of Professor Derek Russell-Davis to come forward to give evidence about the precise issue which I have to deal with on the issue of lesbianism. Professor Russell-Davis is not only an eminent consultant psychiatrist and charted psychologist, but a distinguished Emeritus Professor of Mental Health at the University of Bristol. He has vast experience in the field of family care and also lesbian households.[2]

The judge accepted the expert evidence of Professor Russell-Davis, who summarised the research evidence of the 1983 British study undertaken by S Golombok et al,[3] dealing with the psychosexual development of school-age children of lesbians, and who had also looked at peer-group relationships. Russell-Davis also referred to American research, undertaken by Green et al,[4] in 1986, which looked specifically at whether children of lesbians were more likely to be teased at school.

The conclusion of the expert witness as reported in the judgment was that the sexual identity of the boy would not be affected by growing up with a lesbian mother – ie that he was not more likely to grow up homosexual. Nor was there any evidence that he was more likely to be teased or ostracised at school. Russell-Davis indicated to the judge that he had made 'a special study' of this area and had found that children were more likely to be teased because of physical characteristics. He also stated that, in his experience,

> it is rare for children to show an interest in the background of the parents of other children, and that in fact, children are far more tolerant of their classmates' background and parents than most people give them credit for.

Russell-Davis also disagreed with the welfare officer's assessment that 'the mother had not given sufficient thought to [the child's] future development and the effect of bringing him up within a lesbian relationship.' Russell-Davis interviewed the mother and thought that she had 'been well informed' and 'had thought deeply about the issue'. He emphasised that

> little weight should be given to the effects of the mother's lesbianism; the court should have regard to the quality of parenting in all other respects, and the quality of the parenting of the mother was excellent.[5]

This expert witness also disagreed with the welfare officer over her assessment that the boy needed to live with his brother and sister on the basis that siblings should be kept together. He stressed the importance of the bond between a mother and a child at a young age which should not be broken as this could damage his development. He further felt that where there was more than a five-year gap between siblings their 'needs diverge'.

Having detailed the expert's evidence in the report, the judge did not accept that custody should go to the father on the CWO's second point: that another custody application would be made for the child in two years' time. The judgment stated: 'I must assess what is in the interests of M now and, as I can see it, his future development.'[6]

In the final summing up, where His Honour Judge Callman awarded joint custody to both parties and care and control of the youngest boy to the mother, he stated plainly that he preferred the evidence of the expert witness Russell-Davis to that of the welfare officer and that

> I do not consider that there is now, or in foreseeable years to come, any special risk that would really entitle this case to be resuscitated on the grounds of this boy living in a lesbian household, so long as his general care remains as it is at present ... and so long as the parents continue

to realise the importance of real and meaningful contact between the children and [the child] with his father.[7]

However, the judge constructed a distinction, which he considered significant, between the lesbian couple involved in the case and 'militant lesbians'. He highlighted the fact that both women had been in previous heterosexual relationships and were 'private persons' who 'do not believe in advertising their lesbianism and acting in the public field to promote their lesbianism'. He stated:

> this is another matter of principle: what is so important in cases is to distinguish between militant lesbians who try to convert others to their way of life, where there may well be risks that counterbalance other aspects of welfare and are detrimental to the long-term interests of children either in relation to their sexual identity or corruption, and lesbians in private.[8]

Such a statement does raise grave concerns for lesbian mothers who may be campaigning for their rights or are activists in the feminist or lesbian communities. It also continues to give support to myths that lesbian mothers can unduly influence their children's own sexual identity.

Fortunately, this case has been largely overshadowed by the Court of Appeal case of *C v C*, which took place between August and October 1990.

C v C[9]

This case involved three hearings for the care and control of a seven-year-old girl. The first hearing was in a provincial County Court, where the judge awarded care and control to the mother. The second was held in the Court of Appeal, where the judges decided that the case should be reheard in the Family Division of the High Court. The final High Court hearing, before Mrs Justice Booth, was reported in 1992.[10] At this hearing care and control were returned to the mother.

The importance of *C v C* is that it hinged on expert evidence on the effects of children growing up in lesbian households. The Appeal Court had ruled that the County Court judge had not given significant weight to 'the lesbian factor' and that expert evidence should be called for. As a result of the strong precedent set by this case, experts were no longer regarded as necessary in a number of subsequent cases as the issue had been adequately dealt with by caselaw.

A significant factor which led to the final judgment in the mother's favour was the father's and stepmother's strong disapproval of the mother's lesbianism and the effect it was felt their overt anti-lesbianism would have on the child.

In *C v C* the mother and father had been married for just over a year, when the relationship broke down and the father left the matrimonial home. The girl, who was only a few months old at the time, remained with her mother.

In 1987 when the couple divorced, a consent order was drawn up giving care and control to the mother, with the father having 'reasonable access'. In 1988 the father remarried and the mother, who began work as a prison officer, questioned her sexual orientation and came out as a lesbian to her ex-husband. Having left the prison service, the mother moved to a different area and set up home with an ex-prisoner.

When the child was on an access visit to her father in October 1989, her mother and partner were evicted from their flat. They asked the father if he could allow the child to stay until they found other accommodation. The father subsequently refused to return the daughter and applied for an order for care and control on the grounds of the mother's lesbian relationship.

At the county court hearing in June 1990 the welfare report made no recommendations about whom the child should live with. The judge apparently felt that in his coming to a decision on custody, the mother's sexual orientation was not significant, although he took into account the view that the child would be exposed to disapproval of her mother's lesbianism if custody were granted to the father. In reaching his conclusions on granting custody to the mother, the judge gave weight to the fact that the child would be aware of the mother's lesbian relationship, whether or not she lived with her, and would find it difficult to deal with the issue if living with her father. He also concluded that the child had a stronger bond with her mother than with her father, and that this should not be broken.

The appeal case brought by the father was heard by judges Glidewell and Balcombe, who held that the County Court judge had not given sufficient weight to the lesbian relationship. No expert evidence had been given, and it was stated that the judge had not given enough thought to the child knowing about her mother's relationship at an early age. It was also felt that he had not considered the effect on the child when her school friends discovered the relationship, and the social disapproval that might result.

Despite their concerns about the original decision, the Appeal judges made it clear that

> the fact that the mother has a lesbian relationship with Ms A does not of itself render her unfit to have care and control of her child ... It is, however, an important factor to be taken into account in deciding which of the alternative homes which the parents can offer the child is most likely to advance her welfare. The judge did not give proper consideration to this factor.[11]

Additionally, both judges made it clear that they thought the heterosexual nuclear family was the preferable alternative. LJ Glidewell stated that he regarded it

> as axiomatic that the ideal environment for the upbringing of a child is the home of loving, caring and sensible parents, her father and mother. When the marriage between father and mother is at an end, that ideal cannot be obtained ... [the court's] task is to choose the alternative which comes closest to that ideal.[12]

There were also two subsidiary factors which they felt had not been taken into account, even though they might not be of much weight. These were that the mother's partner had a conviction for violence and that the child had only been at school for a few weeks when living with her mother and had since settled into a school near to her father's house, remaining there for nearly a year.

Making the point that neither judge had heard the original witnesses, as is common in Appeal cases, they made the somewhat unusual order for a rehearing so that a judge in the Family Division of the High Court could 'decide afresh the proper weight to be given to all the factors'.[13] They also invited the Official Solicitor to act as a guardian ad litem, a person appointed to represent the child, and asked that he consider whether to call appropriate expert evidence on behalf of the child.

This decision indicates a high degree of unease amongst the Appeal judges. Clearly they could find no reason to allow the father's appeal but were reluctant to return the child to her mother and the mother's partner. In essence, ordering a rehearing and calling in the Official Solicitor was removing the decision from their hands.

In the Family Division rehearing, Mrs Justice Booth heard expert evidence from Dr Michael King, a psychiatrist who had expertise in 'issues relating to homosexuality' and had studied these 'in depth'.[14] King gave evidence on three counts in relation to the mother's lesbianism. First, he was

of the opinion that a child living in a homosexual environment would not be encouraged into a homosexual lifestyle, and would not be more likely than a heterosexual child to become homosexual.[15]

In giving his evidence he referred to the 1983 British research.[16]

Second, he thought that the child might be more likely to suffer discrimination from her peers if living with her mother. However, he stated that children are teased for many reasons, and teasing in this area was not inevitable. Crucially, he did think that the child would cope better with the discrimination if she lived in her mother's household, and the mother could

explain the situation and other people's potentially discriminatory attitudes.

Third, he had no concerns that the child would be involved
in sexual activities in the mother's household, and he pointed
out that paedophilia has no connection with homosexuality.[17]

Though the expert evidence on lesbian issues contributed
to the final outcome, it was not the only consideration. King
interviewed the child about where she wanted to live on two
occasions, separately with each parent, and both times she
had said she wanted to live with her mother. The strength of
the mother-child bond was therefore an important factor.
This contrasts with the earlier ROW survey findings where
the views of children who had lived with their mother had
not been taken into account. However, by the time of this
hearing the principles enshrined in the welfare checklist of
the Children Act were in force, and therefore weight had to
be given to both the child's view and maintaining the status
quo.

The court considered the criminal record of the mother's
new partner, who had a history of drug use. However, as she
had been successfully rehabilitated and was working in a
position of trust this was not considered prejudicial against
her. Whilst the stability of the mother's relationship was un-
tested, it was felt that even if they separated, the child would
still have a close relationship with her mother.

Another more significant factor was the father's and stepmother's disapproval of the mother's lesbianism. The fact that
the father had informed most of his friends about the mother's
sexual orientation was not considered to be in the child's best
interests. The father had only reluctantly agreed to allow the
child staying contact (staying overnight with the mother) if
he retained residence. The stepmother had been totally
opposed to mother-child staying contact because of the
mother's lesbian relationship. Because of this strong disapproval towards the mother it was felt:

> The problems the child faced could not be faced happily
> and honestly without potential damage to her in her
> father's home. They could only be faced by her in the

mother's home with the real possibility that she would be little harmed by the mother's way of life.[18]

Mrs Justice Booth ultimately came to the same conclusion as the first judge. The only new element in the final hearing was the fact that expert evidence had been called.

The appeal and rehearing meant a long period of delay and stress for the child and mother, based on the anti-lesbian views of the father, who brought the Appeal case, and the Appeal Court's decision to send the matter back for rehearing on dubious grounds.

Both this case and *B v B* highlight the judiciary's most common concerns in lesbian residence disputes. However, these precedents illustrate that, while a mother's lesbianism is still taken into account, it is other factors such as the child-mother bond, the ages of the children and their wishes that now tend to determine the final outcome. *C v C* gave so much weight to expert evidence that it is unlikely such evidence will need to be called in future cases involving lesbian mothers.

Re H[19]

The only reported case on a joint residence application by a lesbian couple was in the High Court under section 8 of the Children Act 1989. The case, *Re H* (a minor) (1993), involved a lesbian couple applying for residence of a child they were hoping eventually to adopt.

The case arose in unusual circumstances because it involved surrogacy arrangements, whereby a friend who was pregnant and did not wish to care for any more children agreed to have the baby for the couple. The local authority had become involved, as they opposed the women's application for private fostering of the child on the grounds that one applicant had a criminal record and the other a history of mental illness. Due to the local authority's opposition to the fostering application, the couple applied to the Family Division of the High Court for a residence order.

At the time of the residence application the child was eight months old and had been cared for by the lesbian couple since birth. During that time it was stated that the care of the child had been 'entirely satisfactory'. The judge stated:

> The fact that they are lesbians does not, according to the evidence that I have heard, make it any less likely that the placement will succeed than if they were an ordinary heterosexual couple.[20]

The case in fact hinged more on factors around the couple's suitability to care for a child. These included concerns over the surrogacy arrangement and the proximity of the natural mother, the history of the applicants' broken relationships, one of the applicant's history of mental illness and the couple's apparent lack of insight into the difficulties the child would face when she grew up because of the circumstances of her birth.

The judge finally awarded an interim residence order to the applicant without a history of mental illness, although it was recognised that both applicants would still have care of the child. He also suggested that counselling help should be made available to them so that they could understand any emotional difficulties the child might face in the future. An investigation was ordered to be undertaken by the local authority into the child's circumstances under section 37 (4) of the Children Act 1989. In addition, the judge made a prohibited steps order in the form of an injunction stating that the natural parents should have no contact with the child.

This case is of interest for lesbians insofar as it demonstrated that being a lesbian is not in itself a bar to obtaining a residence order, even where there is no biological link with the child.

More recently, publicity has been given to lesbian co-parents obtaining joint residence orders. One such application involved a non-biological co-parent of a child;[21] another case dealt with mothers who each had a biological child and who obtained join residence orders for each other's children.[22] This appears to be an area of law which is relatively unproblematic for lesbians.

56   Valued Families

NOTES

1. *B v B* (minors) (1991) 1 FLR 402.

2. (1991) 1 FLR 404–5.

3. Susan Golombok, Ann Spencer and Michael Rutter, 'Children in Lesbian and Single-Parent Households: Psychosexual and Psychiatric Appraisal', *Journal of Child Psychology and Psychiatry* 124, 4 (1983), pp551–72.

4. Richard Green, et al, 'Lesbian Mothers and their Children: A Comparison with Solo Parent Heterosexual Mothers and their Children', *Archives of Sexual Behavior* 15, 2 (1986), pp166–84.

5. (1991) 1 FLR 410.

6. (1991) 1 FLR 409.

7. (1991) 1 FLR 410.

8. (1991) 1 FLR 410.

9. *C v C* (a minor) (custody: appeal) (1991) 1 FLR 223.

10. *C v C* (custody of child) (no. 2) (1992) 1 FCR 206.

11. Balcombe, LJ (1991) 1 FLR 233.

12. (1991) 1 FLR 228.

13. Glidewell, LJ (1991) 1 FLR 233.

14. (1991) 1 FCR 214.

15. (1992) 1 FCR 207.

16. Susan Golombok, Ann Spencer and Michael Rutter, 'Children in Lesbian and Single-Parent Households: Psychosexual and Psychiatric Appraisal'.

17. (1992) 1 FCR 207.

18. (1992) 1 FCR 208.

19. *Re H* (a minor) (s. 37 direction) (1993) 2 FLR 541.

20. (1993) 2 FLR 545.

21. *Re C* (a minor) (residence order: lesbian co-parents) (1994) *Fam Law* 468, discussed in (1994) *Fam Law* 643.

22. *Pink Paper*, 11 October 1995.

PART 2

Advice and strategies

CHAPTER 5

LEGAL ADVICE AND REPRESENTATION

Obtaining good legal advice is important for any aspect of lesbian parenting. By 'good' advice we mean not only advice informed by a thorough knowledge of family law, but which is also supportive of lesbian parenting. Despite the changes that have occurred in judicial responses to lesbian parents, ROW still hears from women who have consulted otherwise reputable law firms and been advised that because they are lesbians, they stand no chance of winning residence orders in respect of their children. Clearly such lawyers are either letting their prejudices overrule their legal knowledge or they are still working from 1970s' legal judgments.

One mother interviewed for this book described going to a local solicitor:

> I went to a male solicitor in the high street, who told me whatever happened I wouldn't get the children, because of my lesbian relationship. As a result of this bad advice I eventually left the matrimonial home without them. Then the father made it more and more difficult to get them back.

COSTS AND LEGAL AID

Legal aid is a Government scheme providing, depending on income, financial help towards legal costs. Unfortunately, legal advice from a solicitor is expensive and only those who are on low incomes qualify for legal aid.

Currently, full payment of legal costs is only available to women who are on income support or have an income at the level of income support or below. Anyone who has an income above this amount still has to pay a contribution towards legal costs, even where they might qualify for some legal aid. Depending on the amount of work needed to be undertaken by a solicitor and whether the case goes to court, this can come to a considerable sum. At the time of writing there are proposals to reduce legal aid still further, so when seeking legal advice a woman should always check what the legal aid position is and the costs charged by her solicitor.

It is also worth women making initial enquiries as to whether they are eligible for advice under the Green Form scheme, which covers free advice and letters written by the solicitor at the beginning of a case. The Green Form scheme may be phased out in the future, however. If there is more work needed than is covered under the Green Form financial limits or if the case has to go to court, a further application has to be made for legal aid, which can take up to eight weeks to come through.

An additional complicating factor is that not all firms of solicitors undertake legal aid work, as this is contracted out by the Legal Aid Board, and whilst some are contracted to supply legal aid family work, these solicitors may not have the expertise to deal with lesbian parenting cases and/or related issues such as immigration.

Another issue that has to be considered is that legal aid is cash limited, so that there may not be legal aid support for all of the work in a complex case.

The Family Law Act 1996

The provisions relating to divorce which are contained in the Family Law Act (FLA) come into force in January 1999. This Act brings in new legal aid provisions for mediation. Under the FLA, it is proposed that most disputes over family matters should be resolved through mediation to save expensive court costs, unless there are good reasons why disputes cannot be settled in this way. The Act requires that persons seeking legal aid to resolve family disputes attend a meeting with a mediator, who will decide whether mediation is appropriate for resolving their particular issue and also whether it could take place without any party 'being influenced by fear of violence or other harm' (s. 29 (3) (f)).

We suggest that lesbian parents seek legal advice before attending a meeting with a mediator. (See also Chapter Six on strategies on divorce and separation.)

Costs of going to court

Where a woman receives partial or no legal aid, her legal costs will be expensive if she engages the services of a solicitor to represent her. Some disputes can be resolved through negotiations between solicitors, and in these cases, costs will be lower than having to go to court. Going to court may also involve engaging the services of a barrister, unless a woman's solicitor is qualified to undertake advocacy work or she represents herself (see below). Engaging a barrister increases the costs of a case. Costs will also multiply if an expert witness needs to be called or there are a number of court hearings.

The statutory charge

Where a woman has been granted legal aid and she recovers or preserves any money or property as a result of legal proceedings, the Legal Aid Board is entitled to recover the costs of the proceedings from any settlement she receives. She should ask her solicitor for more details about this statutory charge and when it has to be paid.

It is not yet clear whether this charge will also apply to finance and property received as a result of mediated agreements, and again information should be sought about this from a legal advisor.

Obtaining free advice and reducing legal costs

Initial free legal advice can be obtained from a number of organisations, including ROW. ROW provides a free legal advice telephone service to women and has specific expertise in giving advice to lesbian parents, whatever their circumstances and the issues involved. It can also refer women to solicitors who undertake legal aid work and have expertise in the area of lesbian parenting. ROW can also put women in touch with solicitors who may be willing to give some initial free advice over the telephone. Other organisations such as Citizens Advice Bureaux (CABs) and law centres also provide free advice in some areas of the law such as housing, and in the future may be funded to provide legal advice in other areas. (See the section on Resources for contact information.)

It is also possible for legal costs to be reduced by women undertaking some of the legal work themselves (such as collecting witness statements where a case needs to go to court) or by taking legal advice and then acting for themselves rather than being represented by a solicitor or barrister. Given the legal complexities outlined elsewhere in this book, women should think carefully before deciding to represent themselves and should consult with organisations such as ROW/CABs before committing themselves to this course of action.

In uncontested cases where, for example, lesbian co-parents are applying for a joint residence order, it is possible for women to represent themselves without incurring unnecessary costs. For more about this see Chapter Seven, Lesbian co-parenting.

Another way that a few lesbians have raised funds to help fight contested 'custody battles' is by holding a benefit or social event specifically for this purpose. Obviously, this option is only open to lesbians who live in a supportive community.

INJUNCTIONS

ROW is producing a self-help guide for women who need to seek court orders (injunctions) to protect themselves and/or their children from domestic violence. (The guide will be available during 1998.) For more on injunctions, see Chapter Eleven.

FINDING A SUITABLE SOLICITOR

Where lesbians are seeking legal advice they need to be reassured that the solicitor they are using understands and is sympathetic to the issues involved. ROW is able to provide names from a national list of recommended women solicitors.

Before engaging a solicitor, a lesbian parent may wish to check the following factors. Most can be checked over the phone:

• Does the solicitor provide legal aid advice/representation?

• Is the lesbian parent eligible for legal aid, and what financial contribution will she be required to make?

• Will the lesbian parent qualify for initial free legal advice and assistance under the Green Form scheme?

• Where a lesbian parent does not qualify for initial free advice, she should ask for details of the solicitor's fees for different aspects of her work – eg hourly rate for advice, writing letters, preparing a case for court if necessary. If the woman decides to instruct the solicitor, she might wish to ask if she can be billed on a regular basis, to keep some control over the costs.

• To have full confidence in her legal advisor, a mother will need to know that the solicitor is not anti-lesbian or homophobic and is supportive of lesbian parents. She may wish to ask whether the solicitor has any doubts about lesbianism or lesbians raising children.

- Where a lesbian mother is coming out of a heterosexual relationship with the father of the child, she needs to know whether the solicitor has had any experience of residence/ contact disputes in which lesbian issues have been raised, including the following:
  - different strategies that can be used in such disputes (as described in Chapter Six);
  - the psychological research and expert evidence that can be used in this type of case (as described in Chapter Three);
  - previous cases and judgments;
  - other issues, such as domestic violence/child abuse, that may form part of the case.

- Will she be undertaking the work herself, or using an assistant?

- When can she be contacted? (Lesbian parents need to keep in regular contact with their solicitors and find out how the case is progressing. On the other hand, solicitors are very busy and do not like being constantly telephoned. A mother therefore needs to negotiate how to keep in regular contact without appearing to pester the solicitor. Asking this question early on will give an idea of how this can be organised.)

A lesbian parent may be able to do some of the work on her case herself to reduce costs. She should discuss how she can do this with the solicitor.

TELLING A SOLICITOR

In the past many women felt, with justification, that if there was a court case looming they needed to keep their lesbianism a secret. The situation is different now; the courts' view of lesbian mothers has moved on. Moreover, a solicitor needs all the facts in order to give good advice and to represent the client properly.

If the father is aware that the mother is a lesbian it would be unwise to deny it, since it will undoubtedly come out at some stage. If the father is not aware but the child is, or knows that the mother spends a lot of time with her new friend, the child may let something slip and the father will make use of this during the case. The courts are not sympathetic to a woman who has apparently lied.

If a woman has not come out or is not certain of her sexuality or feels that her lesbianism is something completely separate from the rest of her life, she may want to talk to someone, for example a ROW adviser, about whether or not she needs to tell her solicitor.

Once a solicitor has been told by a woman that she is a lesbian, and the case is in dispute, the solicitor will not be able to keep that information from the court or from the court welfare officer. The solicitor must not mislead the court and in a case involving children has a positive duty to inform the court of any matters which may affect the child's welfare. Lesbianism is seen as one of those matters. A solicitor can certainly not advise a client to lie. If a woman decides to discuss the matter with her solicitor but feels that he or she is not sympathetic the woman may wish to consult another firm or seek advice from ROW.

CHANGING A SOLICITOR

At the time of writing, if a lesbian parent is dissatisfied with her solicitor's work she can change to another solicitor, whether or not she is in receipt of legal aid. In the future a woman who is legally aided may not have this option because of the proposed changes to legal aid funding. Before taking any decision to change solicitors, be clear as to why you are making this choice. Sometimes solicitors have to give you advice which you might prefer not to hear but which is accurate.

It is important to find a new solicitor before sacking the old one, as something important may happen in the interim.

USING A BARRISTER

If a case has to go to court a barrister may be needed, although some solicitors can also undertake legal representation in court. ROW has a list of barristers who are experienced in dealing with disputes where lesbianism is an issue.

CONFERENCES

There should be at least one meeting with the barrister before the case comes to court. These meetings are known as conferences, and usually take place in the barrister's offices (chambers). A conference is attended by the woman, a solicitor's representative and the barrister (also known as 'counsel'). At a conference to discuss the case, a barrister cannot speak to anyone who is a potential witness, other than the client. Therefore if a woman's partner is going to be called as a witness, the barrister will not be able to talk to her about the case.

A conference enables any problems to be ironed out and the evidence to be thoroughly discussed. It is often useful to make a list of concerns before the conference which the woman can then raise with the barrister. A woman can make suggestions and the barrister should listen to these.

A woman may have friends or relatives who want to speak on her behalf or who the woman thinks might be useful to her case. She should ask her barrister if they can give evidence. If the barrister says they are not necessary, a woman should ask why. The barrister may feel that all the witnesses are saying the same thing, which will simply increase the length and cost of the hearing. The barrister may be concerned because sometimes witnesses say things which a woman had not expected to hear and which may not help her case – the more witnesses there are the greater the risk. If the friends and relatives are not to be called as witnesses, a woman should suggest that she show letters of support to the court welfare officer.

A lesbian parent should discuss with her barrister how she wants her case conducted and what are the important issues for her. For example, she may not want the father to be cross-examined about his own sexual behaviour, or she may want questions to be asked about his living accommodation. A woman may want to refer to things which happened in the past, perhaps three or four years ago. She should explain why she thinks these matters are relevant. However, courts are often reluctant to deal with things which happened many years ago, unless they are part of a pattern of behaviour which is relevant.

A barrister may seek to find out what, if any, issues are open to compromise, and a lesbian mother needs to be clear about what compromises, if any, she is prepared to make.

A barrister should explain what the procedure in court will be, who will speak first and when the witnesses will be called.

If a barrister disagrees with the mother's suggestions, she/he should be asked to explain why. It is quite appropriate to ask if the barrister has had experience of this type of case or what her/his expertise is. It is important to remember that a barrister's skill shows itself in many ways: knowledge of the way the courts work, ability to negotiate with other barristers and advocacy in court. The barrister may not be a person a woman would want as a friend. Taking that into account, if a mother is not happy with her barrister she can ask the solicitor to instruct someone new, although this may involve additional costs.

CHAPTER 6

KEEPING THE CHILDREN – STRATEGIES ON DIVORCE AND SEPARATION

This chapter looks specifically at the issues that may arise for women who realise they are lesbians whilst married or living within a heterosexual relationship. It addresses the legal and related issues that need to be considered in splitting up with a male partner when there are children involved.

KEEPING THE CHILDREN – THE GOOD NEWS

One of the first things mothers will need to consider is the children and who they will live with. The good news is that the courts' attitudes towards lesbian mothers has changed. On the whole, they are now prepared to act on the belief that being a lesbian should not prevent a woman bringing up her children. Where a woman has identified as a lesbian or is in a lesbian relationship, this does not mean she has to give up looking after her children unless she chooses to do so.

The guiding principle of the judiciary is the welfare of the children and what is considered to be in their best interests. Whilst the most recent reported judgments (described in Chapter Four) still consider that the fact of a mother's lesbianism must be taken into account, this is only one of the many factors to be considered, along with others such as the stability of the child's living situation and which parent is most capable of meeting the needs of the child. Each case is considered on its own merits, and much will depend on the mother's and father's circumstances and how both of these are presented. The court may also decide that it is not in the children's interests to make any order, and will then expect the parents to sort out arrangements themselves.

If it comes to a court hearing, there will usually be a welfare report, and the attitude of the court welfare officer (CWO) investigating the case, as well as that of the judge hearing the case, is important.

BEING PREPARED FOR THE DISPUTE

Getting good legal advice

Getting the appropriate legal advice is essential for lesbian mothers who may become involved in disputes over the residence of the children. This advice should preferably be sought before any discussions are had with the father. The importance of getting such guidance cannot be stressed too strongly.

How and where to obtain good legal information is discussed in Chapter Five, and contact information for helpful organisations is listed in Resources.

Deciding to keep the children

If a mother has decided that she wants to keep the children living with her, she should attempt to take them with her if she leaves home. Once she has left the children, it may be much harder for her to get them back. In residence disputes, the courts take into consideration with whom the children are living at the time of the separation and for how long they have remained there since. They recognise that stability is very important to children and may not be prepared to overturn the current living arrangements, unless there are good reasons for doing so. They will, however, consider all the circumstances, and if a mother does have to leave the children for some reason, the courts may still award her a residence order. In this situation she should try to retain as much contact with them as she can, and should seek legal advice as soon as possible.

Taking decisions about coming out as a lesbian

Telling the father

Where a woman has not already told the children's father she is a lesbian, or is in a lesbian relationship, it can be to her advantage not to tell him until after the separation has taken place. However reasonable a father has been in the past, he is likely to have a strong reaction to her lesbianism and could make life very unpleasant for her. The decision about when to tell him can be made after the separation.

If the mother has moved out to live with someone else and the children are still seeing their father, it can be very difficult to conceal the relationship, as he will be likely to find out from the children themselves. Also, a judge will not look favourably on a woman deliberately misleading the court about her lifestyle.

Where a mother is living alone, she needs to weigh up the advantages and disadvantages of concealing her lesbian identity from the father. It can be very stressful to have to live a life of concealment for any period of time. Moreover, if the father later finds out a mother is a lesbian after the arrangements have been made for the children, he could use this as a reason to apply to the courts for a residence order. However, this does not necessarily mean that the courts would make an order in his favour, especially since a woman could argue that she knew the father would give the children inappropriate information which would be harmful to them.

Telling a solicitor

For a discussion about telling a solicitor, see Chapter Five.

Telling the children

What and when to tell the children will depend on the circumstances, their ages and understanding. Where a mother is moving out with the children to live in a lesbian relationship, she will need to explain this new situation to them. Further, if a mother's ex-partner knows about the relationship and is unhappy about the situation, he is likely to tell the children in order to try and turn them against her.

Younger children tend to be more accepting of different relationships than older ones, particularly young adolescents, who may be more ambivalent because they fear the disapproval of their friends. (See Chapter Three for more on this.)

Deciding where to live

Once a mother has taken the decision to separate from her partner, she needs to consider whether to stay in the shared home or move out. If she is married or cohabiting she may have the legal right to stay. The law in this area is quite complex and depends on whether or not she is married, the type of housing tenure, whether it is owner-occupied or privately rented and whether her name is on the property deeds or rent book. She will need to take advice on these issues, either from ROW or through a solicitor. If the father is violent or has threatened violence, she may be able to obtain an order excluding him from the home. (Domestic violence issues are covered further in Chapter Eleven.)

In reality, it is often very difficult for a lesbian mother to remain in the family home unless her ex-partner is prepared to move out. Separating can inevitably cause hostility, and this may increase if the father knows that the mother is a lesbian. He may refuse to move out and blame her for making this necessary. Even if she obtains an order removing him from the home, this may not be effective in keeping him away. ROW has found that fathers often react very emotionally and express high levels of anger on learning their partners are lesbians. In this situation many lesbian mothers feel that they have no choice but to leave.

When a lesbian mother decides to move out with the children, the best strategy is to plan this in advance, before the father is informed. This might be particularly important if a woman is moving in with a female partner. In an interview for this book, two lesbian mothers with several children between them who were leaving their respective husbands to live together said:

> We planned to rent somewhere not far from the children's schools and set this up before we told the children's fathers. But there was still a month in between before we could move. Within this month we were both subject to a lot of physical aggression and harassment, so we wished we had been able to move immediately.

NEXT STEP – GETTING DIVORCED

Women who are married will need to consider getting divorced. The Family Law Act 1996 (FLA) changes the entire procedure and is due to be implemented in January 1999. As the new legislation will make the entire process longer and more difficult, women considering divorce should commence proceedings before this date.

The following discussion outlines the current legal position as well as the new procedures.

Under current law, in order to obtain a speedy divorce, it has to be demonstrated that the marriage has irretrievably broken down by reference to one of the following facts:

- One of the parties has committed adultery (ie has had sexual intercourse with someone of the other sex).

- One of the parties has behaved in such a way that it would be unreasonable for the other party to go on living with him/her. This is usually known as 'unreasonable behaviour'.

- One of the parties has been deserted.

Otherwise, a divorce can be obtained only after two years of separation between the parties if they both consent; or after living apart for five years if one party does not agree to the divorce. No one can petition for divorce unless they have been married for at least a year.

Note: There may be complicated transitional arrangements for divorces that are based on the grounds of a two-year/five-year separation prior to the implementation date of the FLA, but which were filed shortly after January 1999. In these circumstances, seek legal advice.

The unreasonable behaviour category is very wide, and usually grounds to meet the criteria for divorce can be found under this heading (eg domestic violence, or failure to help with childcare and/or housework). If a woman's partner knows she is a lesbian he can divorce her on the ground of 'unreasonable behaviour'. This takes approximately six to nine months if all goes smoothly.

Either party can initiate divorce proceedings, and it is possible for a woman to undertake her own divorce to save on legal costs. See the Resources section for information on where to obtain divorce forms and explanatory leaflets. However, we suggest that a lesbian mother may wish to seek legal advice before undertaking this, particularly if there is likely to be a dispute over children, property or finances.

From January 1999 divorce will become more difficult as new procedures come into effect. Where children under sixteen are involved, a divorce cannot be obtained before a period of eighteen months has elapsed from the time when a person first seeks to initiate a divorce.

Not only do the arrangements for the children have to be finalised before a divorce order will be granted, but also any financial and property matters have to be agreed. This differs from the current law, where financial and property matters can be dealt with after the divorce.

Exceptions to the 18-month waiting period

There are two important exceptions to these rules which

could be of particular significance to lesbian mothers and which would allow a divorce to be obtained within 12 months. These are: (1) where there is proof of domestic violence (ie there is a court order for non-molestation or an occupation order – FLA 1996 s. 12 (a)) – and (2) where the court is satisfied that a longer delay would be significantly detrimental to the welfare of any child of the family – for example, where child abuse has occurred (FLA 1996 s. 7 (12) and schedule 1). There are also certain other circumstances where the financial arrangements do not have to be agreed before a divorce order can be made. These include where the other partner is being obstructive and where for reasons beyond the control of the applicant or the other party the financial position cannot be determined (FLA schedule 1).

Starting the divorce process

Attending an information meeting

Under the new procedures, anyone wanting to divorce will have to attend a compulsory information meeting. How such meetings will be organised and who will provide the information has not been determined in the Act and will be specified by Government regulations prior to implementation. At this meeting, information will be provided on how to seek protection from domestic violence, the use of mediation to resolve disputes, where to obtain legal advice, information on legal aid, and an explanation of the new divorce process.

Making a statement for divorce

After attending the information meeting, an applicant will have to wait three months before she can make an application to a court for a divorce. This application is now called a statement of marital breakdown. The statement only has to say that the marriage has broken down. It does not have to give particular grounds for the divorce, and therefore does away with the idea of divorce being brought about by the 'fault' of the other party. In the statement the applicant will have to state that she is aware of the period of 'reflection and consideration' (the 15-month delay between filing the statement and applying for a divorce order or, if the exceptions above apply, the nine-month wait) and that she wishes to make arrangements for the future.

Unless both partners are making a joint application for a divorce (in which case they can attend an information meeting together if they want to), the statement of marital breakdown will then be served on the other partner, who will also have to attend an information meeting. The other partner can contest the divorce and the proposed arrangements for the children, finances and property.

Where agreement has been reached

If both parties agree the arrangements for the children and any property and financial assets, and the court has received a declaration of the arrangements made, then a divorce order will be granted 15 months after the statement of marital breakdown was first filed.

Where arrangements for the children have been agreed, however, the court will have the power to intervene and to exercise any powers under the Children Act 1989 if it thinks the arrangements made do not serve the child's best interests (FLA 1996 s. 11). Whilst the same power existed under the old divorce law (Matrimonial Causes Act 1973 s. 41, amended by the Children Act 1989 schedule 12), the FLA strengthens these powers. The FLA states that the court must have particular regard to the wishes and feelings of the child and *the conduct* of the parties in relation to the upbringing of the child, and focus on the principle that the welfare of the child will be best served by having regular contact with those who have parental responsibility for the child and with other family members. (For a detailed discussion of the presumption of contact see Chapter Two.)

The introduction of the clause on conduct of the parties is worrying for lesbian mothers, as it appears to be reintroducing the idea of 'fault' by the back door. However, it is not yet clear how the courts will use or interpret such powers to intervene, and this will not become clear until caselaw clarifies the position.

DISPUTES OVER ARRANGEMENTS FOR THE CHILDREN

Where there is disagreement over the arrangements for the children, under both current and new divorce law provisions, either partner can start proceedings for a residence or contact order. These applications are governed by section 8 of the Children Act 1989 (CA), and thus are sometimes referred to as applications for section 8 orders.

Mediation

Under the FLA provisions, coming into effect in January 1999, where one partner has started proceedings for a residence or contact order the court *may* give a direction stating that the parties must attend a meeting with a person 'chosen by the court' to receive an explanation of mediation facilities and the opportunity to 'take advantage of such facilities' (FLA 1996 s. 13). This will be a joint meeting unless one of the parties asks to meet the mediator separately. Lesbian mothers may well feel it is more appropriate to ask for a separate meeting, particularly where the father is hostile or she fears violence from him.

Before attending the meeting, a lesbian mother will also need to consider whether mediation will help to resolve the dispute. Where the father is particularly hostile to her keeping the children because of her sexual orientation, or where she fears harassment, intimidation or violence from the father during the mediation process, she or her legal representative will need to be able to make a case as to why mediation is unsuitable in her particular circumstances. (These and other problems associated with mediation are discussed in Chapter

Two.) She will need to show why there is a necessity for the court to make an order rather than expect the parties to reach a mediated settlement. (Domestic violence issues are discussed further in Chapter Eleven.)

Under present legislation, a woman who is applying for a residence order may also be expected to enter into in-court mediation with a court welfare officer (CWO) during the court proceedings. This can be a stressful experience, as it was for one lesbian mother interviewed for this book:

> I agreed to enter mediation, after the welfare officer had done her report, even though the report was favourable to me. I did this to show I was a reasonable parent and that I was prepared to try and work things out with the father, in the best interests of the children. Unfortunately he would not accept that the children wanted to live with me and spent the whole time abusing me, because I was a lesbian. He did not come over in the mediation sessions as a reasonable and sensible parent, and I think this was to my advantage. But I had to go to these sessions three times. If I had not stood firm, I might just have given in, because he was just trying to wear me down, and the whole thing was extremely stressful. We ended up having to go to court anyway, so it was just a waste of time.

The FLA also introduces the idea of children entering the mediation process to express their own wishes and feelings (FLA 1996 s. 27 (8) (b)). At present, in residence disputes involving children who are old enough to voice their opinions, their views are sought by court welfare officers. In terms of good practice, the CWO should meet the child independently of the parents, so that the child is not placed under extra pressure by the presence of one or other parent. Occasionally children will be brought to court to express their opinions during conciliation appointments.

A lesbian mother will need to talk to her legal advisor and weigh up any advantages of entering mediation. She also needs to bear in mind that she could be refused legal aid, when the FLA provisions come into effect, if she is unable to demonstrate that mediation is inappropriate in her case.

Residence orders and parental responsibility

Where parental responsibility is shared

Where a woman has had children within marriage she continues to share parental responsibility with the father after the divorce (CA 1989 s. 1). Parental responsibility means that either parent can take independent actions or make decisions about the children when she or he is with them, without consulting the other parent, providing the parent is not acting contrary to a court order. If the mother has a residence order for the children, for example, the father could not 'kidnap' them or remove them to live abroad.

Prohibited steps and specific issue orders

A mother can prevent an ex-partner from taking actions related to the children by applying for a prohibited steps or a specific issue order. A prohibited steps order (PSO) is granted against a parent to stop him or her exercising parental responsibility over a clearly identified aspect of a dispute. An ex-parte order (ie in an emergency when the applicant applies to court and the judge makes an order without the other party being notified or having an opportunity to be represented) can be obtained rapidly and is used, for example, to prevent a child being abducted and taken abroad.

A specific issue order (SIO) relates to one particular aspect of a child's upbringing which cannot be agreed upon by the parents, such as changing the child's surname.

The situation for unmarried women

Women who are not married have sole parental responsibility for their children, but a mother can make a legal agreement with the father and grant him parental responsibility. The unmarried father can himself apply to a court for parental responsibility, and in any case if the court grants him a residence order, parental responsibility is an automatic consequence. He is also able to apply for a contact order. Where a father is making an application for any section 8 order, a mother should seek legal advice as soon as possible.

Having to leave the children

Even where a mother may have had to leave the children with the father, she could still obtain a residence order in her favour, particularly where the children are young or they express a strong wish to live with her. In this situation she should try and keep as much contact with the children as possible and apply for a residence order as soon as she can. If the father is refusing face-to-face contact she can apply for an interim contact order whilst she is waiting for the residence application to be heard.

Deciding whether to apply for a residence order

There are circumstances when a mother may wish to apply for a residence order to formally settle the question of where the child will live. However, there can be disadvantages in going to court, both in terms of the expense involved if the mother is not legally aided, and emotional stress. There may be considerable delays between making an application and the hearing, even though the CA 1989 s. 1 (2) refers to the principle that delay in determining the matter is likely to be prejudicial to the child. How rapidly the hearing occurs will frequently depend on the father's response and the speed of filing his paperwork at court. Other factors to be considered are whether the mother feels that an out-of-court agreement can be reached and finalised with a legally binding consent order drawn up by the parties' solicitors. It is also wise to be aware that the court may take the opportunity to make a contact order in the father's favour, or even award him residence.

Out-of-court strategies

Many disputes over children – from issues of residence to questions of who should have the child on special occasions and festivals – are settled out of court, not through mediation but through arm's length negotiations between the solicitors acting for the parties involved. Such negotiations have the advantage of protecting the mother from intimidation and ensuring her interests are represented, as well as allowing a cooling off period where the parties do not have to meet face to face. In disputes with lesbian mothers the father may initially oppose the children living with her, on the grounds of her lesbianism.

In ROW's experience, fathers often change their minds about seeking residence of the children when they realise the costs of going to court, and/or the practicalities of actually looking after the children themselves. In negotiations, a good solicitor should point out these disadvantages to the father as well as the fact that he is unlikely to obtain a residence order purely on the basis of the mother's lesbianism. Additionally, there may be other concerns which can be bargained with, such as property and child contact.

Even if it is agreed or ordered that the mother should have residence, the judge will expect the father to be allowed reasonable contact, unless exceptional circumstances such as child abuse exist. However, a mother should not feel forced to agree to contact arrangements which put her own or her children's safety at risk.

An out-of-court agreement can be formalised by the court making a consent order. If no formal order is made but the agreement is broken by one person, then an application for an order should be made.

GOING TO COURT

An application for a residence order can be made at any time after separation, or after divorce. It can be heard in a Magistrate's Court, County Court or the Family Division of the High Court. Where the application is part of the divorce proceedings it will be heard in the County Court or the Family Division of the High Court.

If it is clear that the parents will not reach an agreement, it could be to the mother's advantage to apply for an order, because in some circumstances she can choose the court at which the case is heard. It is often better that a case is heard in the Family Division of the High Court, as judges will have greater awareness and/or experience of disputes where lesbianism is an issue. Provincial County Court judges may be more prejudiced, although this is becoming less of a problem. However, restrictions on the legal aid fund may mean that payment is not available for a hearing in the High Court unless a woman's solicitor can put forward compelling reasons why this is necessary.

The court welfare report

Once an application has been made for a residence order, a court welfare report is usually ordered. The welfare report is very important because the judge should take it into account in making his/her decision. Although some judges do disregard the report, it is far more usual that they will follow the report's recommendations. The report can make specific recommendations and should always state the wishes of the children. Sometimes the report makes no recommendations, leaving the decision entirely to the judge's discretion.

The welfare checklist

Where a mother makes an application to the court for any section 8 order the court's decision is governed by the welfare principle (as discussed in Chapter Two) laid down in CA 1989 s. 1. Decisions based upon this principle are informed by the welfare checklist, which states that the court 'shall have regard in particular to:

a. the ascertainable wishes and feelings of the child concerned (considered in the light of [her] age and understanding);

b. [her] physical, emotional and educational needs;

c. the likely effect on [her] of any change of circumstances;

d. [her] age, sex, background and any characteristics which the court considers relevant;

e. any harm which [she] has suffered or is at risk of suffering;

f. how capable each of [her] parents, and any other person in relation to whom the court considers the question to be relevant, is of meeting [her] needs;

g. the range of powers available to the court under this in the proceedings in question' (CA 1989 s. 1).

The last point refers to the fact that the court is under a duty to consider whether it would be in the best interests of the child *not* to make an order. Alternatively, the court's powers extend to making orders for which no application has been made – eg a contact order – if it is considered to be in the child's best interests.

What a court welfare officer will be investigating
A court welfare officer (CWO) will visit the homes of both parents and will talk to the mother and her partner (if any) and the children. The CWO will also interview the father's new partner, if he has one, and may talk to other close relatives who are involved with the children. The CWO will mainly be concerned with the factors listed in the welfare checklist. There are no hard and fast rules about areas of investigation, but a survey of CWOs involved in investigations with lesbian mothers showed that they focused on the following core issues:[1]

• the ability of each parent to care for the child and to put the child's needs before their own;

• the relationship between all the parties involved;

- the atmosphere in both homes;

- work and childcare arrangements;

- any conflicts which might arise;

- the wishes of the child;

- the mother's lesbianism.

The mother's lesbianism may not be considered important at all, or may be given a high priority, depending on the particular CWO. In general it would appear that CWOs are less prejudiced than in the past and have a greater awareness of psychological research about lesbian mothers and their children. A mother's solicitor is able to provide research information to a CWO and should be prepared to do so if she feels it is necessary.[2]

Another issue considered by CWOs is domestic violence. Where there is the threat of domestic violence from a mother's ex-partner, a CWO should take account of this and investigate its effects on the children. The officer should be told of the existence of any injunctions against the father and should include this information in her/his report. However, CWOs often view domestic violence as something that has happened in the past, rather than perceiving it as an ongoing threat. They can therefore fail to take it into consideration, particularly when making recommendations about contact arrangements.[3]

One lesbian mother who had a recent welfare report prepared in her case described the CWO's visit:

> The welfare officer came to our home and she talked to me and my partner separately. She asked each of us about how we viewed ourselves and the children, and how we managed looking after them, as we have a number of children between us.
>
> She then talked to the children in a group and asked them about what they felt about home and school. She

talked to the older children on their own (aged 9 and 10) and asked where they considered home. She also visited the father's home when they were on a contact visit and asked them again where they considered home in front of the father, so that she could see that they weren't just being pressurised by me. They said home was with their mum, both times. Her report did not really focus on the lesbian issue at all, it just talked about the relationship between my partner and me and how supportive it was.

Whilst it is not good practice to seek children's views in front of their parents, this is an example of a fairly unbiased approach by a CWO conducting an investigation.

Where a welfare officer does demonstrate bias against lesbianism, either in the way she/he carries out the investigation or in the report itself, this can be challenged in court. In some cases a new report has been ordered to be undertaken by a different officer. The report can also be challenged through the use of expert evidence.

Preparing for the CWO's visit and report
A lesbian mother is more likely to convince the judge to agree the children should live with her where she can demonstrate the following factors which relate to the welfare checklist (the checklist appears on pp81–2; the parts to which each factor relates are shown below in bold):

- The children are already living with her and are settled in their (new) home (c).

- The children are happy living with her and are able to express this to a court welfare officer (a, b). Great weight is now placed on the children's wishes, even for children as young as seven.

- She has a 'discreet' lesbian life-style – ie she is able to demonstrate that she does not 'flaunt' her lesbianism in the neighbourhood and is not involved in persuading others to be lesbians (b, e). (See also *B v B* 1991, discussed in Chapter Four.)

- She can show that she is able to put the children's interests before her own (b, f). This could be interpreted by the court to mean that she is willing to enter mediation with the father or to agree to him having reasonable contact arrangements with the children, but see comments above on arrangements which endanger personal safety, or where there is a risk the children could be neglected or physically or sexually abused if the father has contact (and see Chapter Eleven). Remain aware that showing any anti-male bias is not regarded favourably by the courts.

- Her accommodation and childcare arrangements are appropriate for the children (b, f).

- Where a lesbian mother lives with her partner, she will need to demonstrate that their roles and responsibilities have been thought out, as has the nature of her partner's relationship with the children. She will also need to show that any new relationship, particularly where the partner will be involved with the children, is stable (f).

- That she has explained any relationship with a partner to the children in a manner suitable to their ages and understanding, and in a way which helps them deal with any social prejudice (b, f).

- That she can, if necessary, produce a few 'respectable' heterosexual friends/relatives who support her and testify to the children's well-being in living with her (b, f).

Whilst a court will consider all of these factors, not all of them will be given the same weight.

Whether negotiating an agreement out of court or presenting her client's case at a hearing, a good solicitor should be able to highlight the advantages of the mother's application in relation to the welfare checklist. Tactics could also include raising undesirable aspects of the father's character or behaviour, such as drug abuse, criminal convictions and undesirable sexual behaviour.

Dirty tricks

In order to revenge themselves on their ex-partners, a few fathers have alleged that lesbian mothers have sex in front of the children. Whilst very few CWOs and judges would believe this, a lesbian mother needs to be able to refute such assumptions before they arise by asserting that she would not wish her children to see any inappropriate sexual behaviour. This should not mean she cannot share a bed with her partner. It still occasionally happens that a judge may try and put conditions on a mother's residence or contact order stating that she and her lover should behave 'appropriately' in the presence of the children. Such conditions should be strongly challenged by a woman's legal advisor, as this could be interpreted by the father as meaning that the children cannot witness a kiss or the couple showing any form of affection to each other. It can be clearly argued that all parties should behave 'appropriately' in front of children, and the fact that such conditions are never imposed on heterosexual couples merely reflects ignorance and prejudice about lesbians.

We have also heard of a recent case where a father asserted that because they were lesbians, either the mother or her lover would sexually abuse the children. Whilst this is clearly challengable by the use of research evidence (such as that discussed in Chapter Three), in any case where such allegations are made, doubtless the CWO will investigate.

Does the sex of the children make a difference?

Some lesbian mothers fear that because they have sons they will have less change of obtaining a residence order. Research – discussed further in Chapter Three – shows, however, that boys receive male influences from a number of sources. In any case, in residence disputes it is more important to be able to show that children have interests that are conventionally regarded as appropriate to their gender. Such evidence is usually obtained through the CWO's visit.

The hearing

The hearing is attended by the judge, the legal representatives and the mother and father. Before the hearing, each side will have submitted statements about why they think they should have the children. This will also include their reasons for thinking their ex-partner is an unsuitable carer. During the court hearing a mother will have to give evidence, and she may be cross-examined by her ex-partner's barrister, which can be distressing. Her partner may also have to give evidence and be cross-examined. The court hearing will take place in private and a mother's partner, but not friends, may be allowed to listen to the proceedings.

Court procedure

If it is the mother's application she is the applicant. Usually the applicant's barrister speaks first and gives an outline of the case to the judge. Then, usually the CWO is called to give evidence and is asked questions by the judge and by the barristers. Then the applicant is called. The applicant's barrister asks her questions (examination-in-chief) and then she is cross-examined by the respondent's barrister. The applicant's barrister then asks some final questions (re-examination). The judge may ask questions at any time. After the applicant has given evidence, her witnesses are called and are questioned in the same way. Then the respondent's 'case' starts and he is called to give evidence. His barrister asks him questions, he is cross-examined by the applicant's barrister and then re-examined by his own barrister. Then his witnesses are called. If there are any expert witnesses they will be slotted in according to their availability.

When all the evidence has been called, the barristers make closing speeches to the judge. They will sum up the evidence and highlight their strong points and respond to any concerns the judge might have. This is the time when they will refer to earlier cases. The judge will then 'give judgment' and make the order.

Previous cases

In disputes over residence of the children, each case is considered according to its own facts. This means that one case cannot necessarily be used as a precedent for another. Nevertheless previous similar cases are often referred to by judges in making their decisions. A woman's representative should therefore be able to refer the judge to previous cases involving lesbian mothers. (Recent caselaw is discussed in Chapter Four.)

Expert evidence

Expert evidence is where expert professionals in their field are called upon to provide a report and/or to give evidence to the court. (This is separate from the CWO's report.) In the case of lesbian mothers, the expert witnesses are usually psychiatrists or psychologists who are familiar with the research and are able to present this to the court. They may also conduct their own independent assessment of the mother, her new partner (if any) and the children. This can involve assessing the mother and in some cases her partner's caring abilities, the nature of the mother-child relationship, and the mother's understanding and ability to help a child deal with any social prejudice that might result. Any assessment undertaken will be presented to the court.

Expert evidence is now less important than in the past, as a mother's legal team can and should refer the court to previous judgments where such evidence has been presented (see Chapter Four). However, it may still be necessary to call experts if a welfare report is thought to be biased against the mother.

A mother should discuss with her legal representatives whether there is a need for expert evidence in her case, and weigh the benefits of this against the costs involved. In any circumstances her lawyers should be familiar with both the precedents using expert evidence and favourable research findings.

Other evidence

It can help a lesbian mother's case to have evidence from other parties such as concerned grandparents, friends or 'respectable' people from her local community. This evidence can be submitted in the form of statements which testify to her character, caring abilities and/or standing in her local community. In order to reduce the cost of her legal fees, the mother can take these statements herself, after seeking her solicitor's advice.

A person who makes a supporting statement will need to attend court as they may be called to give evidence.

THE COURT ORDERS

The most usual order a judge will make is an order for residence to one party and reasonable contact to the other. Occasionally the judge will make a joint residence order, specifying the times when the child should live with the mother and with the father. A mother should not agree outside court to a joint residence order unless this is what she wants. She should make it clear in her evidence why she objects to such an order – eg it would unsettle the child, or the relationship between the parents is not good enough to make it work. However, it may be suggested by the mother's lawyers in a case where the alternative would be that the father would obtain sole residence. In that case the mother should think hard before objecting. Joint residence orders often only work if the parties are living near each other. The children's own needs and wishes also need to be considered in these circumstances.

Contact

Reasonable contact is usually expected for the party without the residence order. Occasionally this may be defined by the court. 'Reasonable' contact can be as much as every weekend and half of the school holidays.

What happens if a mother does not obtain a residence order?
If the mother is not granted a residence order, she should be given reasonable contact. It may be possible for her to return to court later to reapply for a residence order. There usually have to be good grounds, involving a change in circumstances, for a variation to be made in the original order.

Much will depend on the children's wishes. Where they are plainly unhappy living with the father, these may be grounds to apply for a variation of the order. Once a child has reached age 16, courts will not usually permit a residence order application, as the child is considered old enough to decide with whom he or she wishes to live.

If the court is satisfied that a child below age 16 has sufficient understanding to apply for a variation of residence order, permission can be granted for the child to apply to court (CA 1989 s. 10 (8)). However, courts do not approve of children making an application where they feel it has been inspired by a parent.

Appeals
It is possible to appeal against the original residence order. However, the Appeal Court is reluctant to overturn decisions made in the lower courts unless they feel that the original judge has failed to take into account all of the factors in the welfare checklist, has made a decision which is clearly wrong, or new evidence which was not available at the original hearing has come to light. In order to appeal, however, the

mother will need the judge who heard the case to grant her leave to appeal. Her barrister should therefore ask for leave to appeal immediately after the judge makes his or her order. It may not be possible to appeal the decision, but this is a preliminary step which should always be taken. Then the barrister can go away and consider the judgment and see if there are grounds for an appeal.

It may be difficult to obtain legal aid for an appeal, and a mother should seek legal advice before considering this step.

Applying for contact where a mother is not living with her children

If a mother gives up or loses residence of her children, she can apply for a contact order at any time, particularly where the father is refusing her reasonable contact. A welfare report may be ordered by the court if the father is opposing contact on the grounds of her lesbianism.

A father's contact

A father who has agreed to the mother keeping the children can also apply for a contact order. In some circumstances new demands for contact may be made by the father when he is being pursued by the Child Support Agency for maintenance of the children. It is worth noting that even if evidence exists of the risk of abuse by a father, a court may order supervised contact.

Where a mother fears that a father will behave inappropriately with the children during contact, she can ask the court to impose conditions on the contact order (CA 1989 s. 11 (7)). In some circumstances she can apply for a prohibited steps order (PSO).

Maintenance issues

The Child Support Act 1991, and its implications for lesbian parents, are discussed in Chapter Two.

Fears that a father will make or increase demands for contact which could cause harm to the children are not accepted by the Child Support Agency (CSA) as a valid reason for non-cooperation. Absent fathers also pay less child support where they have the children to stay overnight or where they have to travel to see them, making it likely that fathers being pursued for child support will increase their demands for contact.

Refusal to cooperate with the CSA can mean that a woman's benefits are reduced by 40 per cent within six weeks of her refusal to authorise the CSA to pursue the father.

Appeals

Where a woman makes a case for exemption and she is refused, she can appeal. However, her appeal may not be heard before her benefit is reduced.

In any appeal against a CSA decision a woman *must* instruct the CSA if she does not want her address/details revealed to an ex-partner; if she does not take this step within 14 days, parties to the appeal (for example, on challenging a maintenance assessment made) will receive full details of each other's circumstances.

Women not on benefits

Women not on benefits have a choice as to whether to claim maintenance for the children from the father. If they decide to do so, they now have to make these claims through the CSA. At the time of writing these claims are dealt with last, and it can take many months for a voluntary maintenance claim to be dealt with. A mother will have to pay the CSA a fee if she wants it to collect maintenance on her behalf.

Assessment of child support

Campaigns by fathers' rights groups have reduced the maintenance an absent parent has to pay in child support even if he is very wealthy. No absent parent has to pay more than 30 per cent of his/her net income. There are also a number of allowances which can be claimed to offset against the CSA assessment. A mother can appeal against an assessment if she feels it is too low and does not reflect the father's true income.

Mothers who do not have their children living with them

will be assessed in the same way as an absent father. If a mother is dependent on benefits a small amount of maintenance will be deducted from her income, unless she is disabled, has other dependent children living with her, or shares care of her children for a substantial proportion of the week.

Other maintenance and financial matters

In some circumstances it is possible to obtain other financial payments over and above child support payments through court orders. A mother should seek legal advice about this if it is relevant.

NOTES

1. Moira Steel, 'Lesbian Custody Disputes and Court Welfare Reports', *Social Work Monographs*, University of East Anglia, Norwich, 1990.

2. The psychological research evidence is discussed in detail in Chapter Three. Copies of the relevant research reports mentioned above can be obtained from the ROW office, tel: 0171 251 6576.

3. Marianne Hester and Lorraine Radford, *Domestic Violence and Child Contact Arrangements in England and Denmark*, Policy Press, Bristol, 1996.

CHAPTER 7

LESBIAN CO-PARENTING AND HOUSING ISSUES

Co-parenting roles can vary from equally shared mothering to helping out with the children on a regular basis. More and more lesbians are enjoying the challenge of co-parenting, whether by having children with a partner through self-insemination, adopting or fostering or by becoming involved in co-parenting with a lesbian who already has children. This chapter looks at the legal and related issues involved in co-parenting and at measures that can be taken to help deal with some of the problems that arise.

There are many positive aspects to co-parenting for both the children and their carers. Children can benefit from having two or more mothers and where the co-parent also has biological children they receive the benefit of having other sisters and brothers. Being able to share the caring role means parents have more time to themselves and can also share the problems of bringing up children.

Difficulties can arise from co-parenting, however. These often come to the surface when a relationship ends and co-parents separate. Problems can also arise over decisions about the children, or on the death or incapacity of the biological mother.

In law, non-biological carers have no legal status as parents unless they apply to the courts for such recognition. This situation gives the biological mother considerable power. Even in co-parenting situations where there are no biological parents involved and a couple adopt a child, there can be difficulties as only one of them will be recognised as the adoptive parent. Thus there is always a power imbalance in relation to children.

This chapter looks at some of the ways these power imbalances can be addressed and at what action co-parents can take to prevent and resolve disputes, both within the relationship and on separation, in order to protect both the best interests of the children and themselves as carers. It also addresses issues about housing for lesbian co-parents.

CONSIDERING DIFFERENT TYPES OF CO-PARENTING RELATIONSHIPS

Co-parenting relationships can range from co-mothering where two women share equally in looking after the children and the responsibilities for them, to relationships where one parent does most of the caring and the other or others help out. Sometimes co-parenting can be shared between more than two women. Many women only consider the possibility of co-parenting with a lover, but there are other possibilities, such as co-parenting with a friend or friends, which can avoid some of the complications which may arise between lovers when the relationship ends.

Working out thoughts and feelings on these issues can be difficult. A book called *Considering Parenthood* addresses the issues that lesbians face in this area and can help clarify them.[1]

CO-PARENTING AND THE LAW

The law in relation to children is governed by the Children Act 1989, which has made it possible to recognise, in law, the caring role of non-biological co-parents. Co-parents can now acquire parental responsibility (PR) with a biological mother by applying for a joint residence order under section 8 of the Children Act. (For a fuller discussion on the Children Act, see Chapters Two and Six.)

A lesbian co-parent, in acquiring PR, can share making

major decisions about a child's life with the biological mother, take independent decisions about the child when the biological mother is ill or not available, and take a child abroad on holiday without the birth mother.

Women who live together and who both have children born through donor insemination can acquire PR for each other's children by both applying for joint residence orders with the other partner.

Parental responsibility

Most applications for joint residence orders made by lesbian co-parents are when a child is born through donor insemination and there is no father with PR. There have been a number of these cases, usually where the donor is unknown.

Where a woman states that she knows the donor, however, the court may direct that he become a party to the proceedings and give his permission to the application, even though this is not strictly necessary as he does not have parental responsibility for the child.

Where a father has parental responsibility

In certain circumstances it may be possible for a co-parent to acquire PR through a joint residence order when a father also has PR. ROW is not aware of any cases where this has happened at the time of going to press. In this situation the law states that the father must agree to the application, or the person applying for a residence order must have lived with the child for three years, or the court must grant leave to apply for such an order.

It is probably unlikely that a lesbian co-parent would be granted a residence order in these circumstances unless the father did give his permission, even where she had lived with the children for three years.

Applications in these circumstances will be much more

complicated than those in which there is no father with PR. Before such an application is considered, we suggest that legal advice is sought from ROW or elsewhere.

Where there is no father with parental responsibility
A joint residence order can be applied for at any time after a child has been born, providing that the biological mother gives her permission.

In order to gain a joint residence order, the advantages and benefits to the child need to be stressed, rather than the rights of the non-biological parent. In a very few cases where joint residence applications have been made by lesbians, an independent person, known as the Official Solicitor, is appointed by the court to represent the interests of the child. His/her opinion is an important factor in contributing to the court's decision to grant an order. If a child is old enough she can apply for her own representation, although this is discouraged by the courts.

All hearings for such applications take place in private in order to protect the child. However, in a couple of cases the women involved chose to talk to the press after the case in order to demonstrate the possibility of lesbians gaining such orders. In one case the judge stated that 'he had the child's welfare as his first and paramount consideration' in granting the order (*Re C* 1994).[2]

In order to save legal fees it is possible for lesbians wishing to apply for joint residence orders to make an application themselves, rather than using a lawyer. We have included a self-help guide on this at the end of this book (Appendix A). Legal aid is unlikely to be given for such applications because they are uncontested.

It needs to be borne in mind that the court has the power not to make an order. ROW is aware of a case where an order was refused because the judge believed it was against the best interests of the child.

*What happens where parenting is shared between co-parents
who do not live together?*
The law does allow for a joint residence order to be made
where 'two or more persons do not live together', in which
case 'the order may specify the periods during which the child
is to live in the different households concerned' (CA 1989
s. 11 (4)). An order of this type was made to lesbian co-
parents in 1994 in Nottingham. A court would consider
granting such an order where the arrangement had been
ongoing for a number of years, it was seen as in the best
interests of the child, and the child wished the arrangement
to continue.

*Could a joint residence order be awarded to more than two
co-parents?*
Whilst the law does allow for this, usually to accommodate
the situation of stepparents, it is extremely unlikely that a
court could cope with the idea of recognising that parenting
may be shared between three co-mothers, even though such
situations exist quite happily in the real world.

*What happens if the relationship between lesbian co-parents
with a joint residence order ends?*
If a co-parent moved out of the shared home, she would
continue to have PR of the children unless an application was
made to have the joint residence order discharged by a court
(CA 1989 s. 12 (2)).

Contact orders

A contact order provides for visiting rights or other forms of
contact with a child. Anyone who has a relationship with a
child can apply to a court for a contact order under section
8 of the Children Act if they have lived with the child for
three years or have the written permission of the parent/s
with PR or have leave of the court to apply for such an order.

The usual CA considerations apply in granting a contact
order. A co-parent who, for example, has lived with a child,

has an established relationship with her and has been involved with her upbringing may be able to obtain a contact order if the biological mother is refusing such contact. A co-parent's child can apply for a contact order to see a 'step-sibling' in her own right if the court believes she has sufficient understanding and grants her leave to make an application. In these circumstances the child's legal representative will first have to apply to the court for leave to make an application for a section 8 order. In some situations the courts have been reluctant to allow children to make their own applications, and legal advice should be sought on this.

PREVENTATIVE MEASURES

Increasingly ROW has been hearing from lesbians who have been involved in co-parenting which breaks down, particularly when a sexual/emotional relationship comes to an end. Many women want to know their legal rights in relation to the children, and some have become involved in expensive and bitter legal battles.

Whilst nothing can prevent the pain that may accompany the ending of a relationship, difficulties may be diminished if the issues have been thought through beforehand and consideration given to how the caring arrangements for children are to be shared and what will happen if the relationship between the co-parents ends. Having to resort to legal proceedings can be costly and can work against both the interests of the children and the women involved.

Making agreements

For those considering or who are already involved in a shared parenting relationship, it can often be helpful to make a written agreement about the arrangements for the children should the relationship end or the biological or adoptive mother become terminally ill or die. Some lesbian co-parents have had such an agreement drawn up in a legal form, with the advice of a solicitor. This does not mean that the agreement would necessarily be legally binding, but it would be good evidence of the women's intentions at the time it was drawn up and could be taken into account by a court. More important, an agreement provides a framework for discussing issues if problems arise.

Issues addressed in such agreements often include:

- How major decisions around the children are made and who has responsibility for making such decisions. Where women are involved in co-parenting a child born through donor insemination, it is also important to document how the decision to have the child was reached.

- What the caring relationships for the children are, eg how much time a child spends with each co-parent. This can be particularly important where co-parents do not live together.

- Where co-parents do live together, what the arrangements would be for looking after the children if the relationship between them ended, eg where each child would live, how much time they would spend with each parent, visiting arrangements etc.

- Reviewing the agreement. As circumstances change, co-parents may wish to review and change the agreement, so periodical reviews need to be built into it.

RESOLVING DISPUTES OVER CHILDREN BETWEEN LESBIANS

Ethical considerations

Unfortunately some lesbian relationships, like some heterosexual relationships, break up in a very hostile way. In these circumstances there is often a temptation to use the children to get revenge on the other partner. Some biological mothers try to use the law to prevent a co-parent and ex-partner having any contact with a child. Similarly, non-biological parents have also been known to make accusations about the character and parenting abilities of the biological mother. Such behaviour can neither benefit the children themselves nor the general situation for lesbian parents who are already under social pressure for raising children without fathers. In our experience of such disputes, arm's length negotiations between the ex-partners can help in resolving disputes over children and other matters such as shared property without having to resort to the courts.

Whilst such negotiations can be carried out by solicitors, this can be an expensive way of attempting to resolve the problems. One partner can be disadvantaged if she cannot afford to pay a solicitor's fees or if one or other partner is not legally aided. Some lesbian co-parents have resolved disputes by appointing a friend to represent their interests and to negotiate with someone appointed by the ex-partner.

What about mediation?

Mediation involves a trained person facilitating a meeting between the partners and attempting to help them reach agreement. ROW is not as yet aware of any organisation which is specifically trained to undertake mediation between lesbian partners. However, as with heterosexual couples, mediation is unlikely to work if there is a great deal of hostility between the partners or there are inbuilt power imbalances between them on the grounds of race, financial circumstances or class.

Mediation and the law
From January 1999, when the Family Law Act comes into effect, if a lesbian parent who qualifies for legal aid seeks legal representation or applies to court to resolve a dispute, she will first be referred to a mediator. The mediator will have to consider whether the case is appropriate for mediation, and if it is decided that it is, then legal aid will be granted for mediation meetings, rather than for legal representation.

MAKING PROVISION FOR SICKNESS AND DEATH

Appointing a guardian

A guardian is someone who can be appointed to care for the children when the mother dies. If she dies while her children are minors, the guardian would then gain full parental responsibility.

Appointing a guardian is very easy. There are two ways to do it: the mother can simply sign and date a document appointing a co-parent to be the child's guardian on her death, or she can appoint a guardian when making a will. (See Appendix B of this book for a guide to making a will.) It is important to review the guardianship appointment from time to time to ensure that the appointed guardian is still able to take on the responsibility.

Sickness and incapacity

If a lesbian mother becomes sick or incapacitated the law automatically entrusts decisions to the nearest blood relatives, leaving partners or friends powerless to make financial and property decisions on her behalf. To avoid this a partner or friend can be given Enduring Power of Attorney (a form for this can be obtained from a law stationers such as Oyez). This should be done before the woman becomes incapacitated.

Financial provision for child/ren and lover

If you contribute financially towards the maintenance of a child and/or another woman, it is a good idea to take out a life assurance policy naming who is to benefit, so that when you die they will receive some money. If you are married and you die without having made a will any money and property you own may go to your husband. If you are divorced or have never been married it will go to your

children. So if you want to make a provision for a lover/
friend you should make a will (see Appendix B).

If you have been contributing towards the maintenance of your lover or her child

If you have not made a will and you were contributing
towards your lover and/or her child's maintenance they may
have a claim over any money or property you leave. Likewise
if your lover or friend dies without leaving a will you may
have a claim over her money or property. You do not have
to be a relative to claim but you do have to show 'financial
dependence'. However, the legal fees could be substantial, so
it is much better to leave a will.

HOUSING ISSUES FOR LESBIAN CO-PARENTS

Lesbian co-parents who share housing must also consider
how to prevent and/or resolve difficulties that occur with
property should the relationship end or should one partner
want to leave the shared home. The law relating to property
is complex and the results of getting it wrong can be very
serious, so it is advisable to take legal advice.

Joint purchase of a property

If co-parents wish to buy property together they need to think
carefully about the type of legal agreement that they enter
into with each other. There are essentially two ways that
people can own property jointly, first as tenants in common
and second as joint tenants. Each form has advantages and
disadvantages, and which is chosen will depend on the
women's particular circumstances.

Clearly, if children are involved, a woman will want to
ensure that her children are provided for in the event of her
death. Neither form of ownership prevents her from doing

this, but advice needs to be taken about the specific circumstances of the women and children concerned before a decision is taken on the best way to do this.

Tenants in common
For many women this is seen as the most flexible form of ownership because it preserves the financial and legal rights of the individual. Tenants in common each own their part of the property separately and have the right to dispose of that share without the consent of the other tenant. Whilst this could lead to problems if a share of a joint home is sold, such issues can be addressed in a contract as explained below.

Tenants in common can also leave their share of the property by will to whom they choose, and it is important that women make a will specifying this. A failure to do so will usually mean that the share of the property will pass to the next of kin. This could obviously cause huge problems for the surviving partner.

Joint tenancy
This type of ownership means that both women own the entire property jointly and severally. This means both that they have to agree over the disposal of it (by sale, will, gift etc) and also that they have joint liability, for example, for the whole of the mortgage. If one partner dies, the property automatically belongs completely to the survivor.

A woman's interest in property can be registered, and advice should be taken about how and when to do this. The advantage of registering an interest is that a court can then be asked to intervene if there is a dispute, such as a refusal by one party to sell.

It should also be noted that a joint tenancy can be changed into a tenancy in common fairly easily, by notification from one tenant to the other in writing. Again, legal advice should be taken.

Legal agreements

The point at which a relationship ends is often the hardest time to try to sort out retrospective rights to the property. This can be avoided or minimised by partners giving consideration at the time they start living together as to what they both want to happen in the future.

It is possible to put agreements reached about property into a legally binding contract. Such a contract could also cover issues such as the financial contributions to be made by each partner. Seek legal advice.

Some issues that women may wish to consider including in an agreement are:

- The amount of the property that each woman owns. This could be reflected in percentage terms or could set out a proportion of the sale value, depending on the financial contributions – for example, capital or mortgage payments – made by each.

- How much each woman will pay towards the outgoings of the property.

- Who will remain in the property if the relationship ends.

- If one woman does move out, whether the other will buy her out and, if so, over what timescale.

- What will happen to the property if the child/ren leave home. Will it be sold, for example, or should part of it be rented out?

Renting accommodation

Women renting from a local authority or a housing association need to safeguard their rights in the event of their partner dying or leaving the accommodation.

Although some local authorities do have equal opportunities policies that recognise the rights of lesbian and gay couples and co-parents to remain in a property after separation or to inherit a tenancy on death, these can be subject to demands for proof of the relationship, which couples may find invasive. The law does not recognise the rights of lesbian co-parents to succession of tenancies.

The best way to ensure both parties have rights in the property is to have both names on the tenancy agreement, creating a joint tenancy. Then, if one partner leaves or dies, the remaining woman should retain rights to the property.

A woman who does not have such legal rights will probably not be able to remain in the property once the tenant has left and will need to apply as a Homeless Person under the 1996 Housing Act. If she has biological or adoptive children, or if she has parental responsibility for children, then she will be considered to be in priority need and will be entitled to at least temporary accommodation. A number of housing associations will also prioritise lone parents, and friends or relatives may be able to provide a temporary place to stay. Property can also be rented privately, although some private-sector landlords will not rent to people with children.

The law on homelessness is complex, and the 1996 Housing Act has brought in considerable changes. At the time of writing it is not yet clear what the precise effect of these changes will be, and a woman should always check her position carefully.

Domestic violence

In certain circumstances a partner or co-parent may have rights to remain in or return to a property (either owned or rented) where she has experienced domestic violence from the other partner. These rights are exercised through applying to a court for an occupation order. Details on how to obtain such orders are given in Chapter Eleven.

Future changes in the law

The Law Commission is currently reviewing the rights of 'unmarried home sharers' and has made efforts to consult the lesbian and gay communities to ensure our circumstances are not overlooked. The Law Commission is particularly concerned about the lack of rights for those who do not have tenancy agreements or any financial investment in a property owned by someone else. The legal position of lesbian home sharers may therefore change in the future.

ThE POSITIVE SIDE OF CO-PARENTING – PARENTS AND CHILDREN

Some lesbians do not want to have children themselves but welcome the opportunity to be involved in caring relationships with children. The benefits and difficulties around the different types of co-parenting arrangements are best expressed by the parents and the children themselves.

In an interview for this book, one lesbian mother described her experience with co-mothering where both women had their own biological children around the same time:

> We had to be incredibly clear about what our expectations were and how we would share the mothering role. We each breast-fed both children and made sure that we spent equal amounts of time alone with them. We gave them the same last name, which was different from either of our own.
>
> We discussed what would happen if we broke up, and agreed that we would still share the children equally. We actually broke up when the children were about five and we knew that we had no right to take away our own biological child from the other mother, even though we might have wanted to. This was as much because of the child's relationship with the other mother as well as our agreement. We both felt we had earned the right to a mothering relationship with the other child.
>
> At times, during and after the breakup, it has been quite a strain to continue in the co-mothering role. The children

spend half a week at one household, and half the week at the other. We share weekends and holidays, but these are flexible, depending on our own and the children's needs. In order for this arrangement to work, we have to continue to live near each other, when one or other of us might have wanted to move to a different area altogether.

We also found we had different attitudes to the way the children should be brought up. We resolved that by agreeing that what happened in our own half of the week was our responsibility. We also agreed not to undermine the other's parenting role.

Even though it has been difficult at times, I feel it has been very positive for the children, and for me it has made all the difference to be able to share the parenting responsibility with someone else; I haven't had that sense of aloneness in mothering children. It also meant that because we had the basic framework there, I was clear about the support I needed from other friends and lovers.

However, another biological mother involved in co-mothering said, in an interview for this book:

I feel that you need to build in some flexibility into your initial agreement. I agreed to co-mother with my partner, who was not going to be the biological mother. Our relationship then ended when our child was only a few months old. At the time I did not feel able to pull out of the agreement, even though I wanted to. I feel now that even though our child has benefited from co-mothering, I should have been able to change the agreement. As the child was so young she had not developed a strong bond with the co-mother, and I don't think it would have harmed her if the relationship had changed.

Co-parenting can also bring surprises, both good and bad. One mother describes a rift between herself and her partner: 'When I decided to have a second child, Jennifer was clear that she did not want to mother another child. At first I was furious, but it helped me to know what I could expect and that I would have to find support elsewhere.'³ Another describes her change of heart: 'I never expected to be an equal parent with C. I thought I'd help out now and then. Once Alexis was born I wanted to be as involved as I could. It was hard for both of us to adjust to my sudden change.'⁴

In interviews for this and other books, the children of co-parents often describe the pleasures of having two mothers. One six-year-old girl said:

> I have two mothers and other kids don't. I feel different. I don't tell most of my friends I have two mothers, but the ones that know think it's nice. I don't tell other kids at school about my two mothers because I think they would be jealous of me. Two mothers is better than one.⁵

A 12-year-old boy described life with two mothers who live apart:

> About a year ago one of my mothers moved out of the house we were all living in, now she lives about a mile away. My brother and I go back and forth between the two houses. It wasn't really that hard when my mothers split up. For a while it was hard to remember where I had left things. And the rules are different in each house. But that was always true as my mothers have different ways of doing things.⁶

A 14-year-old girl interviewed for this book has the benefit of three mothers:

> I've actually got three Mums but I live between two households. There are a lot of advantages because it means I get a wider range of life, and when I have a row, I can talk it through with one of my other Mums. It's nice living with lesbians because it means you get to make choices about your own identity.
>
> All my friends like my Mums, and at school we have an equal opportunities policy about different families so there's no teasing or anything like that. The only drawback

about living between two households is that I sometimes forget things, or I want things from the other house, but it's not a problem really. I love it.

And a 10-year-old boy interviewed for this book described his sadness when his co-mothers split up: 'When my mum split up with Jo, I would have liked to have gone on seeing her, but she didn't come and see me. I miss her a lot.'

NOTES

1. C Pies, *Considering Parenthood*, Spinsters Book Company, San Francisco, 1988.

2. *Re C* (1994) *Fam Law* 468, discussed in (1994) *Fam Law* 643.

3. C Pies, *Considering Parenthood*.

4. C Pies, *Considering Parenthood*.

5. L Rafkin, ed, *Different Mothers: Sons and Daughters of Lesbians Talk about their Lives*, Cleis Press, Pittsburgh, 1990.

6. L Rafkin, ed, *Different Mothers: Sons and Daughters of Lesbians Talk about their Lives*.

CHAPTER 8

DONOR INSEMINATION

Donor insemination offers lesbians the possibility of having children without having a sexual relationship with a man. It also allows women the choice of not having a father in their children's lives. Increasing numbers of lesbians have been having children through donor insemination since the late 1970s. This can be done through self-insemination or by using the services of a specialised clinic.

Self-insemination involves a woman finding a donor or donors, inseminating herself and hopefully becoming pregnant. There are self-insemination groups which a woman can join if she is thinking of having a child through this method. With this method the woman may know the donor. The other method of conceiving a child in this way is to obtain anonymous donor insemination through a clinic licensed to provide such services.

This chapter looks at the legal issues and implications of having children through donor insemination and the issues lesbians need to consider in order to protect themselves and the well-being of their children. Practical information about how to obtain donor insemination can be found from other sources (contact details are given in Resources at the end of this book).

USING A LICENSED CLINIC

Licensed clinics are covered by the Human Fertilisation and Embryology Act 1990 (HFEA). During the passage of the Bill attempts were made to prevent access to donor insemination services through clinics for lesbians and single women, but these were defeated. A concession was made to the anti-lesbian lobby in the Act, which says:

> A woman shall not be provided with treatment services unless account has been taken of the welfare of any child who may be born as a result of the treatment, and any other child who may be affected by the birth, *including the need of that child for a father.* (HFEA 1990 s. 13 (5)) (emphasis added)

The ambiguity in its wording means that clinics have the discretion as to whether they provide donor insemination services to lesbians. Some clinics have ceased to do so, but some clinics still provide this service.

Legal implications of using a clinic

Legally there are advantages to using a clinic – the donor must sign a consent form abdicating parental responsibility, so he has no parental claims on any child born from the use of his sperm. In addition, the donor is anonymous and cannot be pursued for child support or maintenance under the Child Support Act 1991. A child born through this method is considered to have no legal father unless the woman is married, in which case her husband is deemed to be the child's father. If the mother is unmarried, the child is not considered illegitimate as this concept has been abolished in law.

The donor will be screened by undergoing tests for sperm count (for fertility), genetic conditions and HIV infection.

There are practical disadvantages to using clinics, however, which for some women may outweigh the considerations of legal protection. The disadvantages include the cost, which can be very high for each insemination as clinics charge for their services. It can also be more difficult to get pregnant because the clinics use frozen sperm which is less active than fresh sperm. Clinics can also be limited in their choice of donors because they are dependent on donors coming forward to offer their services. This can mean that they offer a limited choice of donors from different ethnic origins. Lesbians with disabilities may also find themselves discriminated against by clinics who may refuse to give them donor insemination.

A child born through anonymous donor insemination at a licensed clinic can, under HFEA section 31, be given minimal information about the donor, primarily for the purpose of finding out if they are related to an intended spouse. The law may change in the future as proposals are afoot for HFEA regulations to be amended so that persons born through anonymous donor insemination will be able to obtain limited information about their father on reaching the age of 18. The proposed information includes eye and hair colour and occupational interests.

SELF-INSEMINATION

There is no law against a woman informally obtaining fresh sperm and inseminating herself. It is not illegal:

- for a woman or a group of women to advertise for donors or for newspapers or magazines to carry advertisements for donors;

- for a self-insemination group to screen donors or introduce them to interested women; or

- for a woman to help another woman to get pregnant, for example by acting as an intermediary in obtaining and delivering fresh sperm.

However, if a self-insemination group were to freeze sperm,

this would be contrary to the HFEA, which forbids the storage, in this case freezing, of eggs or sperm without a licence.

There are a number of practical advantages to using self-insemination. Women do not have to pay the costs of going to a clinic and they have control over the process. They are not subject to the assessment procedures used by clinics which may reject them as unsuitable, and they are also more likely to get pregnant as fresh sperm is used. Self-insemination means that women can also seek out the kind of donor they want through advertising, although this does not necessarily mean that suitable donors will come forward. There are also disadvantages to be considered, including genetic and medical disadvantages, such as the possibility of infection, and the legal consequences. Recent legislative changes have made the situation more complex for lesbians choosing to use self-insemination, particularly where they wish to use a donor they know.

Legal implications of using self-insemination

The two laws that most directly impact on women using self-insemination are the Child Support Act 1991 and the Children Act 1989. Though the Children Act does have positive aspects for women, there are some risks that the biological father could obtain parental responsibility or a contact order due to the central concept of the Act that it is in the child's best interests to have contact with both parents. The Child Support Act is based upon the state's concerns about paying benefits to lone parents and attempting to minimise the fiscal costs of families headed by women. Negative elements of both pieces of legislation are focused around implicit social policies which predicate that a two-parent, heterosexual family is the most desirable form of living arrangement.

Effects of the Child Support Act 1991 when a known donor is used

Where a mother is on income support, family credit or claiming disability working allowance, she is legally required to cooperate in giving information to the Child Support Agency (CSA) about the biological father in order for the CSA to pursue him for maintenance both for the child and for a proportion of the mother's personal benefit allowance. This requirement operates even where the mother may have made a previous agreement with a donor not to involve him in any financial support, as the CSA does not accept such agreements. The Act also applies retrospectively and can therefore affect mothers who have already had children through self-insemination. A woman can refuse to give information to the CSA, but in this case her personal benefit allowance will be cut by 40 per cent for a minimum period of three years unless she applies for and is granted an exemption.

For example, it is possible to claim exemption from having to cooperate if a woman fears that pursuing the donor will cause either herself or her child 'undue harm or distress' (see Chapter Eleven on domestic violence issues). Unfortunately, the fact that the donor might demand contact with the child if he has to pay maintenance is not regarded as an adequate reason to claim harm or distress or for the CSA not to pursue him.

Additionally, a donor obviously cannot be pursued if the mother does not know where he is, although she is legally liable to give what details she has of him to the CSA. Alternatively, some women may have used donors who live abroad and are therefore outside the remit of the Act.

A mother in receipt of the benefits mentioned above will be contacted by the CSA and asked to complete a Maintenance Assessment Form (MAF), which asks for information about the absent parent. If the woman does not wish the father to be contacted she can put her reasons on the form and apply for an exemption to the requirement to cooperate. Prior to applying for an exemption a woman might wish to seek legal advice.

Usually anyone refusing to cooperate will be called to an

interview with a CSA officer (CSAO). It is acceptable to take a legal advisor or witness to the interview. Every CSAO has discretion as to whether to accept a woman's 'good cause' claim that the biological father not be contacted. It is possible to appeal against the CSAO's decision if a woman considers it unreasonable.

The requirement of the Child Support Act make it compulsory for a biological father to be pursued for maintenance only if the mother is in receipt of the benefits described above. It does not apply where a mother is not claiming benefits, as in other circumstances child maintenance applications are voluntary.

The effects of the Child Support Act might mean that potential donors need to consider their position carefully prior to offering their services, and it is as well to discuss all the issues in advance of making any arrangements with a known donor.

Effects of the Children Act 1989 when a known donor is used

Potentially, although it is unlikely, a donor who knows he is the biological father could apply under the Children Act for certain legal rights relating to the child. In principle a biological father has the legal status of an unmarried father, which would allow him to apply for the full range of section 8 orders. Usually only in exceptional cases do courts deny parental responsibility or contact orders to unmarried fathers, even where this is against the mother's wishes. Where a donor has had considerable involvement in the upbringing of a child, he could potentially apply for a residence order. In general, where there is a pattern of ongoing contact and knowledge of biological fatherhood, a court might well order that the donor has contact with the child under the primary principle of the Act that children should have contact with both parents.

Many donors do not wish for any contact or involvement with the child. However, in the experience of a few women who have contacted ROW, some known donors have changed their minds about not wanting to be involved with the child and have made life difficult for these women by attempting to assert their legal paternal rights.

Alternatively some donors, while not wanting contact, are prepared for a child to be given information about them later on. This is an issue that needs to be discussed with the donor at the time. A woman may wish to enter into a formal agreement with a donor as to what is expected by both parties to the arrangement.

Some lesbian mothers may feel that a child born through self-insemination could want to know who the donor is when they are older, or that the children may wish at some point to have contact with him. In this case being able to use a known donor for self-insemination can be a benefit, providing that the donor does not take advantage of the situation to acquire legal parental rights and that he can be reassured that he will not be pursued for child maintenance.

As mentioned above, one way around the complications introduced by the Child Support Act and the Children Act is to use a donor who lives abroad most of the time. Such donors can be contacted through advertisements. Risks in contacting donors this way include personal health and safety considerations. All potential donors should be met in a public place. A major concern is knowing how far the donor is to be trusted to tell the truth about his own health and other situations.

Using an unknown donor via an intermediary
It is possible for lesbians using self-insemination to choose to have an unknown donor by using an intermediary. An intermediary is someone who will collect the sperm and will keep the identities of the woman and the sperm donor a secret. In this case neither the Children Act nor the Child Support Act will apply. As far as the Child Support Act is concerned intermediaries cannot be pursued by the CSA to reveal the name of a donor.

However, using an intermediary can make the process of self-insemination more complicated as the intermediary needs to be able to collect and deliver sperm from a donor when the woman is most fertile. It can also make choosing the type of donor more difficult. A woman will need to be reassured that the donor has been properly screened for infectious diseases such as HIV and for genetic conditions.

Being involved in a self-insemination group can make the process of using an anonymous donor easier. Other women in the group can act as intermediaries, and can also take steps to check the health of donors. One woman interviewed for this book described how this can work:

> The self-insemination group we had used when B was trying to conceive had undertaken to do the vetting of potential donors on behalf of its members. This involved requesting information about HIV tests, family illnesses, the existence of other children by the donor and finding out the motives of the donor. The great advantages of groups like these is that they offer a good deal of control to the women who use them.

Guardianship

In order to avoid the possibility of known donors acquiring guardianship rights, women who have children through self-insemination can appoint a guardian of their own choosing. This is a simple process and is a step all lesbians who have children through self-insemination should consider (see the Appendices to this book).

Conclusion

In conclusion, both the Children Act and the Child Support Act have made it more complex for lesbians considering self-insemination, particularly where a lesbian does not want any involvement from the donor in bringing up the child. The Child Support Act could potentially also mean that fewer donors will volunteer their services.

Co-parenting and donor insemination

Another issue that often arises for lesbians considering pregnancy through insemination is whether to have a child jointly with a partner or friends who wish to be involved in co-parenting and share mothering responsibilities. Some lesbian couples also choose to try and get pregnant at the same time. There are a number of practical and legal issues to be considered in making these choices; these are discussed in Chapter Seven.

The experiences of women who have used donor insemination

There is considerable ideological pressure these days on all mothers bringing up children without men, suggesting that they are failing in their duty towards their children by depriving them of a father or male figure in their lives or knowing their biological origins.

This has not, however, been the experience of a number of lesbian mothers who had children through self-insemination with anonymous donors in the late 1970s. These women's children are now in their late teens. One of these lesbian mothers said, in an interview for this book:

> It all depends how the circumstances of the child's conception are explained. I told my child he was a very wanted child, and he was conceived through a donor, and this was someone I did not know. He therefore has no father. He has the advantage of having two mothers, as I co-mother with someone else who also had a child through self-insemination. He has never shown any interest in finding out who the donor is, or concern about having no father. The important thing is to be open and honest to a child about their origins.

And a 12-year-old boy describes it from his perspective:

> My mom used a donor to get pregnant and I don't know who it is. I don't know anything about him. Right now that doesn't matter much to me . . . Right now I don't have a reason to find out who my donor is. He could be a real

asshole. I think that was part of my mom's decision not to
know the donor; he could be really awful. He could also
be real nice, but it's hard to say.[1]

A 1991 psychological study of 37 lesbian families in the
US looked at behavioural adjustment, self-image and sex-role
behaviour of children aged between three and six. Of these,
17 children were born through anonymous donor insemination and a further five had no contact with their biological
father. None of these children appeared to have psychosocial
difficulties through the absence of a father figure or through
not knowing who the donor was.[2] A similar study is now
being undertaken in the UK.

NOTES

1. L Rafkin, ed, *Different Mothers: Sons and Daughters of Lesbians Talk
about their Lives*, Cleis Press, Pittsburgh, 1990.

2. Susan Golombok, Fiona Tasker and Clare Murray, 'Children Raised in
Fatherless Families from Infancy: Family Relationships and the Socio-
emotional Development of Children of Lesbian and Single Heterosexual
Women', *Journal of Child Psychology and Psychiatry*, in press, 1997.

CHAPTER 9

ADOPTION AND FOSTERING

This chapter looks at the legal issues involved in fostering and adoption by lesbians and includes the experiences of lesbians interviewed specifically for this book who have gone through the adoption or fostering process. Under current law, the only people who can adopt are legally married couples of whom one must be over the age of 21 years, or a single person aged 21 or above. This means that lesbian couples are excluded from adopting *as a couple* and that only one of the partners can be the legal adoptive parent.

WHY ADOPT OR FOSTER?

There are many reasons why lesbians choose to adopt or foster a child. Some consider adoption or fostering a positive alternative to having children themselves. Others have been unable to get pregnant. Some choose to foster children when they have had children of their own. The following are extracts from interviews for this book:

> For me, planning to adopt was a positive choice. I didn't want to have a child biologically, but felt that there was a lot I could offer as a parent to another child or children.

> We decided originally to try self-insemination, but after about a year we found it too stressful and nothing was

happening. So we decided to rethink what we were doing and apply for fostering.

My decision to apply to adopt, rather than having a child without being married, was based on being sensitive to my parents and their position in a close-knit Asian community.

After bringing up our own daughter, we felt we could offer a safe home to a young woman who has been abused, as there is a huge need in this area. As lesbians we know about alternative networks for survival apart from the nuclear family and we felt we could offer a young woman the confidence to live outside of family ties that can harm her.

OPPOSITION TO LESBIANS ADOPTING OR FOSTERING

Whilst lesbians have been quietly adopting and fostering children for years as single women, there has been considerable discrimination against out lesbians doing so. Although there is no legislation which says that lesbians cannot adopt or foster, there have been various attempts to exclude them, including moves in the early 1990s to change the fostering guidelines to the Children Act 1989 and to limit adoption to heterosexual married couples.

Resistance to these moves has come not only from lesbian and gay organisations but also from many fostering and adoption agencies themselves. Unfortunately, the greatest constraint on lesbians choosing this kind of parenthood is the unwillingness of some local authorities and adoption and fostering agencies to consider lesbians as prospective parents, as well as a bias towards choosing heterosexual couples in selecting homes for children. For some agencies this includes a fear of negative publicity from the gutter press, who have managed to acquire personal stories concerning lesbian couples involved in adoption. Others have openly refused even to consider lesbians for fostering and adoption. These have included voluntary agencies such as The Children Society and some local authorities.

Attitudes are slowly changing as increasing numbers of lesbians are recognised as foster or adoptive parents, even though in the case of adoption these numbers are still quite small. New possibilities for fostering have also been opened up as some local authorities recognise the need to find foster placements for older teenagers who themselves identify as lesbian or gay and who may come into care because of their parents' disapproval.

The vast majority of placements where lesbians are considered as prospective foster or adoptive parents involve what the agencies define as 'hard to place' children. This has a very broad meaning and can include a range of categories, from children suffering emotional trauma as a result of sexual abuse to those with learning or physical and mental disabilities. It can include large numbers of siblings who need to be adopted together.

Such a situation has come about not only because there is a preference for placing children with heterosexual couples, but also because of the very small number of babies available for adoption since the 1970s.[1] This has been the result of the wider availability of contraception and abortion, and because being a 'single' mother has ceased to attract the social stigma of previous periods so that many single women choose not to place their children for adoption. In addition, the Children Act 1989 has meant that social work and childcare practices now focus on keeping children with their birth parents as far as possible.

Whilst there has recently been pressure from right-wing 'family values' lobbies to push for legislation that would once again encourage single mothers to give up their children for adoption and to limit adoption to married couples, so far such pressure has not been effective.

ADOPTION THE LEGAL PROCESS

The current law on adoption is set out in the Adoption Act

1976. This may change in the future, and those considering adoption need to investigate any changes before proceeding.

Adopting a child in this country means becoming a child's legal parent. Once an adoption order has been granted by a court, the child's birth parent(s) lose all legal rights and parental responsibilities for that child. In cases of 'open' adoption, contact is retained between a child and her/his birth family in order that all ties are not broken, although the adoptive parents have all the powers associated with a residence order and parental responsibility. A court can make a contact order when making an adoption order, or informal contact can be agreed between the adoptive and birth parents or blood relatives.

The adoption position in this country is different from a number of other countries where legal connections with the birth parents are not totally severed by adoption, and legally the child remains a member of both families.

In considering whether a child can be adopted, the current law requires that

> the courts, social service authorities and voluntary adoption agencies give first consideration to the need to safeguard and promote the welfare of the child throughout childhood, and so far as practicable to ascertain and give due consideration to her/his wishes and feelings. (Adoption Act 1976, s. 6)

New legislative proposals also include a welfare checklist that agencies and the courts must take into account in deciding whether a child can be adopted. The checklist introduces new considerations in regard to the child's welfare, including stating that courts and agencies must consider how a child might be affected by being severed from its original family, both in childhood and later (White Paper 1996 s. 1 (4) (c)). It also requires them to consider the value to the child of those relationships and the wishes and feelings of the birth parents (White Paper 1996 s. 1 (4) (f)).

Ethnicity and culture

The 1976 Act does not specifically mention ethnic or cultural background as an issue to be considered in placements for adoption. The new legislative proposals state that 'the child's age, sex, *background* and any of the child's characteristics which the court or agency considers relevant' (emphasis added) must be taken into account when making decisions about adoption (White Paper 1996 s. 1 (4) (d)). The usual practice of local authorities and voluntary agencies is to attempt to match a child's own ethnic and cultural background with adoptive parents.

Religion

Under the 1976 Adoption Act an adoption agency must have regard to the wishes of the birth parent(s) as to the child's religious upbringing.

The rights of birth parents

Birth parents have to give consent to a child being adopted, but a court can dispense with this on a limited number of grounds. The most commonly used ground is that the birth parent(s) are unreasonably withholding their consent to adoption.

Under current law, an adoption agency can also dispense with parental consent by applying to a court for a freeing order. This overrides the lack of the birth parents' consent and states that the child is free to be adopted. This can take place before there are any specific adoptive parents for her.

Birth parents can give their consent to an adoption order at the same time as consenting to have the child placed for adoption.

Where a child has been placed for adoption but no adoption order has been made, the prospective adopters can return the child to the adoption agency.

The adoption order application can be contested by the birth parents or others. In one case involving a lesbian couple the application was contested by a former foster parent of the child. Caselaw means that details of the adoptive parents, including their sexuality, may now have to be disclosed as information relevant to the making of an adoption order, unless it can be argued that it would threaten the security of the placement and the safety of the child.[2]

This means that in some cases it may be necessary for the birth parents to know that the prospective adopter is a lesbian. This disclosure of information is in line with a move towards more 'open' adoptions, where birth parents are given more information about prospective adoptive parents and an adopted child may be permitted to have some limited contact with a birth parent after the adoption has taken place. This does not necessarily mean that an application for an adoption order by a lesbian will be opposed by the court, since it may well regard it as unreasonable to object on the grounds of a person's sexuality. It is, however, another factor which has to be taken into account in considering adoption as an option.

Where contact with birth parents is totally severed, both birth parents and the child have the right to make contact with each other through the adoption register once the child reaches the age of 18, and if both parents and child give their permission.

Complaints and representations about adoption

One positive aspect of the Government's new proposals is that adoption agencies will have to set up a complaints procedure for prospective adoptive parents, birth parents and adoptive children. This means that those rejected as adoptive parents will have some means of complaining about their rejection.

FOSTERING AND THE LAW

Fostering means caring for children who cannot be cared for by the birth parents and who are usually subject to local authority care orders. It can involve being a foster parent on a long- or short-term basis. In order to be accepted as a prospective foster parent, applicants must be assessed by a local authority in the same way as being assessed and approved for adoption. However, after assessment, the panel does not have to approve specific placements, and there are no requirements for court orders as in adoption. It is also possible for lesbian couples to apply as joint foster parents, and ROW is aware of a few lesbian couples who have been approved jointly by local authorities. The final decisions about placements are made by social workers, but usually the birth parents will be consulted, as will the child.

Who can foster?

The law on fostering is now covered by the Children Act 1989. Government guidance on fostering states that

> it would be wrong arbitrarily to exclude any particular groups of people from consideration. But the chosen way of life of some adults may mean that they would not be able to provide a suitable environment for the care and nurture of a child. No one has a right to be a foster parent. Fostering decisions must centre exclusively on the interests of the child.[3]

This means that lesbians can openly apply to be foster parents, but it does not necessarily prevent discrimination occurring.

Prospective foster parents can apply for specific types of placements. These include long-term foster care, short-term foster care, or emergency/respite care. The two latter categories usually involve fostering children only for short periods of time. Fostering allowances are paid to foster parents, and these vary depending on the type of placement and the age of the children.

Fostering privately

Private arrangements for fostering still have to be approved by the local authority unless the child is a close relative of the foster carer. The local authority must be notified, and they can attempt to stop the fostering arrangement if they do not think it is in the child's best interests. They can also prohibit it if the prospective foster parent or anyone living with her has certain criminal convictions. The only way a local authority's power in this respect can be opposed is to appeal to a Magistrate's Court.

ADOPTION AND FOSTERING IN PRACTICE FOR LESBIANS

By law a person applying to adopt or foster must be assessed and approved as suitable by an adoption and fostering agency or local authority. This is described in detail below. (The situation is less complex if it is a private adoption where the child is related.[4]) Applicants also must be at least 21 before they can be considered as adoptive or foster parents. Police and medical checks will also be carried out on the applicants, and personal references must be supplied. In the case of adoption, the child must live with the applicant for at least 13 weeks before an application can be made for an adoption order – ie after the assessment, approval, and placement processes are completed.

Deciding which partner is the named adopter

In the case of adoption where a lesbian is living as part of a couple, although legally only one of the partners can be the adoptive parent, in practice both partners will be involved in the assessment process. One of the first things that a lesbian couple will have to consider is the issue of who is going to be the adoptive parent, as described by one woman interviewed for this book:

> Having to choose which of you is going to legally adopt can be a very difficult decision if you want to share child-care equally. Even if the decision is taken easily, you don't know what effects it may have later. It creates a power imbalance between you and, if you split up, the partner who isn't the named adoptive parent has no automatic rights to the child.

A lesbian partner who is not the named adopter can apply to share parental responsibility with the adoptive parent through a residence order, under section 8 of the Children Act, at the same time as the adoption order is being sought. If the adoptive parent's sexuality has not been disclosed to the birth parents, it may be advisable to seek a joint residence order once the adoption has taken place. Details of how to do this are discussed at the end of this chapter and in Chapter Seven.

Finding an agency

Having decided to apply for adoption or fostering, the next step is to approach an adoption and fostering agency. In the first instance, for most lesbians, this is the adoption and fostering unit of a local authority. A number of local authorities have equal opportunities policies which state that they do not discriminate against lesbians and gay men, and it is advisable to approach an authority which has such a policy. This does not have to be the local authority where the applicant lives. Despite anti-discrimination policies there is no guarantee that individual social workers involved in assessments will not have an anti-lesbian bias. One of the first obstacles to overcome is finding a social worker who is sympathetic and not heterosexist. As one woman described in an interview for this book:

I contacted a number of local authorities, expressing an interest in adoption, and just went with the first one that responded. This proved to be a mistake and I would advise anyone thinking of adopting or fostering to do some research first to find a sympathetic authority.

Information on authorities that do not discriminate and where social workers may have had some heterosexism-awareness training in relation to fostering and adoption can be obtained through lesbian and gay organisations and networks involved in working around this issue (see Resources at the end of this book).

Saying you are a lesbian

Lesbians who are applying on their own to adopt or foster may find the process easier, as the issue of being a lesbian might never arise. As a woman who adopted an 11-year-old girl said:

The issue never came up. I was asked in general about any future relationships I might have and how I would handle this with an adoptive child and that was all. So I didn't actually have to say I was a lesbian.

On the other hand, lesbians applying as 'single' women may still face heterosexist and/or racist attitudes from social workers. Another woman applying to adopt said:

I felt I was discriminated against as an Asian single woman who was seen as challenging the status quo. The social worker said she was concerned whether a child would fit in and get support from the Asian community because I am single and not part of a heterosexual couple.

Where women decide not to state that they are lesbians, they must consider whether such information is on their medical records and also, since references will be sought, whether their referees will disclose this information. Whilst it is legal not to mention your sexuality, it is illegal to lie or give false information to the authorities, so if asked directly a prospective lesbian applicant must give this information.

Attending an introductory course

Having decided to approach a local authority to express an interest in adoption or fostering, applicants will often be invited to an introductory course which covers the issues involved. Lesbians' experience of such courses have been mixed, depending on the authority running them. One woman, who was in a couple and was applying to adopt, said:

> During the course there were two issues which came up and were stressed as important considerations: one was could you love an adopted child as much as your own? And the other was whether you had got over your wish to have your own child. I felt in my case that this issue was more relevant to the heterosexual couples present who had probably been trying for years to have their own children. For me it is a positive choice to adopt rather than second best.

Another woman who was approved to foster with her partner said:

> We attended a familiarisation assessment group organised for people wanting to foster. Fortunately for us one of the social workers running the course was a lesbian. We were the only lesbian couple present, but there were other 'single' women. We discussed topics in groups such as dealing with racism and homophobia and not using corporal punishment with children. I found it very helpful.

And one woman applying to adopt said:

They don't make it clear when you are attending the course that they are actually assessing you at the same time. I was told that I didn't interact enough with the other course participants who were mainly heterosexual couples. They also didn't like it when I raised questions or when I took a strong line on child sexual abuse and said that abusive fathers shouldn't have contact with their children.

After completing an introductory assessment course, it may take up to a year for applicants to be assessed. Applicants are visited by a social worker and have to fill out a form known as the F form, where they are asked to give very detailed information about their lifestyle, any experience of childcare, financial circumstances, personal philosophy, past relationships, their own family and extended family networks, and friendship and support networks. They also have to provide referees; choosing referees can present difficulties. As one woman planning to adopt said:

Another issue which is more difficult for lesbians is that of who to choose as referees. You need two personal references and these we were told would ideally be from people who have known us as a couple and who have children themselves. Do you ask a lesbian mother to write you a reference? You have to bear in mind that the adoption panel considering your application can be up to 10 people. You may think it would look better if you had at least one referee who was heterosexual, ie making it obvious that you can mix in both communities. Clearly your referees have to know you well, and you may not have the option of choosing a heterosexual referee.

A lesbian couple approved for fostering said: 'We used referees who were both professional lesbians and one was a lesbian mother, and there didn't appear to be a problem with this.'

Having your home assessed and being interviewed by a social worker

Once women have filled out the F form, they will also be interviewed by a social worker and have their home assessed as suitable for children. Women will also need to show they have considered potential local schools for the children and considered what childcare arrangements they will make if they are working.

Lesbians have stressed how important the social worker is, as she/he will be making a report and recommendations to the local panel. A woman with a child placed with her for adoption said:

> Your social worker needs to be understanding, anti-hetero-sexist and have an awareness of the issues involved in lesbians adopting or fostering. She can be crucial in enabling you to get approval as an adoptive parent.

A couple approved for fostering said:

> Our social worker didn't even raise the issue of lesbianism, and we felt it was a good idea for us to raise it ourselves and say how we would deal with any anti-lesbian prejudice or discrimination in relation to any child we fostered.

A woman applying to adopt said:

> I was made to feel very weird by the social worker, because as a black, single woman I was wanting to adopt. It wasn't said directly, but I was made to feel I wasn't 'normal' because I wasn't in a heterosexual relationship. Although having a social worker who has similar ethnic and cultural ties to you can be an advantage, it can also work against you, as it did in my case. At the end of the day social workers have a lot of power. There is no appeals procedure, so who are they accountable to? Social workers vet prospective foster and adoptive parents. I think we should be

able to vet them, to be able to choose a social worker we feel is sympathetic and who we can feel comfortable with.

The panel

Local authorities and voluntary agencies have adoption and fostering panels who approve applicants as suitable prospective adoptive or foster parents once they have been assessed. A panel must include two lay people from outside the authority and a medical advisor. In the case of adoption these panels also have to approve a particular adoption placement.

The final process of adoption takes place in a private hearing in court. High Court adoption applications issued out of the Principal Registry take place at the Royal Courts of Justice, where there are facilities for the prospective adoptive parent(s) and the birth parent(s) and other parties to be present in court throughout the hearing without being seen or identified by any other party in the proceedings.

Considering and getting a placement

The assessment process, including being approved by a panel, is likely to take up to a year. Applicants will have already had to consider what type of placement they want or are prepared to accept. It has already been mentioned that the only type of placements likely to be considered for lesbian couples, or lesbians applying as single women, are what are known as 'difficult to place children' and that this category is very wide ranging. However, very young children are far less likely to come into this category unless they have particular special needs or have been sexually abused. Lesbians are often considered as suitable placements for sexually abused children/young women for obvious reasons. All available children are likely to be experiencing emotional difficulties as a result of their life circumstances.

How soon a placement is made will also depend on whether applicants are applying to foster or adopt and the type of

placement being sought. A lesbian couple who were seeking
to offer a safe home to an abused teenage girl, one of the
categories of young people needing foster parents in their
area, only had to wait a few weeks for a placement to come
up once they had been approved by the panel. A couple
wanting to adopt younger girls had to wait two years:

> We applied to adopt siblings as we thought we would stand
> a better chance of being considered if we agreed to adopt
> more than one child, with a preference for a child of under
> school age. Also we weighed up what we ideally wanted
> and what we would be realistically offered and knew that
> we would only be considered for hard-to-place children.

It can be very stressful waiting for a placement to come
up. After a year, prospective adoptive or long-term foster
parents who have been approved can apply to other local
authorities and voluntary adoption agencies.

Women can also answer advertisements which are placed
in magazines such as *Adoption UK*, the quarterly journal
Parent to Parent: Information on Adoption Services and 'Be
My Parent', produced by the Family Finding Service of the
British Agencies for Adoption and Fostering. The experience
of lesbians who have done this is that it is better to write
rather than phone in response to these advertisements, so
that their situation can be clearly described in writing. If a
local authority or voluntary adoption agency is interested,
again they will want to visit women in their own home.

One lesbian couple described their experience with this
process:

> The whole process is very wearing. Every time a social
> worker shows interest, they have to interview you and this
> usually means taking a day off work. They ask very per-
> sonal questions, such as how you handle conflict and deal
> with disagreements, but you never know what they are
> going to ask. Some of them are very heterosexist. They
> come and interview you, and then say, 'But don't you think
> a child needs a father?', when they can see from your form

that there isn't one. They come into your living room and then can be quite offensive about your situation. You have to be very determined. They can then keep you waiting three or four weeks before they let you know whether they are going to consider you or not.

Where lesbians are applying for adoption, once a suitable placement does come up, it will be discussed with the applicants and they will have an opportunity to see photos/videos of the children. The placement then has to be agreed by the adoption panel, but this can happen fairly quickly. The applicants will then be given the opportunity to meet the children and can withdraw at this stage. They will also meet the current foster parents. This can be difficult as the foster parents may disapprove of children being adopted by a lesbian. However, the prospective adopters should ensure that the social worker works with the foster parents to challenge any anti-lesbian attitudes so that the situation does not arise where an adoption order is being contested on these grounds. In some cases it will also be necessary for work to be undertaken with the birth parents as well. Social workers should also support the children and prepare them for moving to their new home.

Under current law the agencies and the courts must consider the wishes and feelings of the child as far as possible. Under the new proposals a child aged 12 or over cannot be adopted unless she 'freely consents' or the court considers she is incapable of 'giving such consent' (White Paper 1996 s. 41). The wishes of a young child in relation to adoption may be sought through a guardian ad litem – ie a person appointed by the court to represent the interests of the child.

After a transition period when the adoptive parent(s) will meet the children and foster parents several times, the children will finally be moved to their new home.

For lesbians involved in foster care, placements may take place much more quickly. They will meet the child and also usually meet the birth parent. Again, at this stage, they may encounter anti-lesbian prejudice, which they need to be prepared for. Although it is the responsibility of the social workers to work with the birth parents to challenge such attitudes, this doesn't always happen.

SURVIVING WITH THE CHILDREN

Social work support should be available in the first months of an adoption or fostering placement. The children also have their own social worker whom they can contact. Children frequently take a long time to settle in a new home, and the first year or so is often a period of adjustment for both the adoptive or foster parents and the children themselves. Lesbians who are proposing to adopt may choose to wait longer than the statutory 13 weeks before applying for the final adoption order to see if the children will settle.

The settling time is not necessarily easy. A woman with children placed with her for adoption said: 'Nothing can prepare you for how hard it is going to be, although two years on I still think it is worthwhile.' One woman involved in joint fostering described her experience:

> We had one placement which hasn't worked out. It's very tough and distressing in lots of ways ... but we still have some continuing contact and time has enabled us to adjust. We decided to continue because the need to provide safe foster care for young teenage women is so great.

THE RIGHTS OF THE NON-ADOPTIVE PARENT

A lesbian partner whose name is not on the adoption order may wish to apply for a joint residence order with the adoptive parent who holds parental responsibility for the child. She can do this if the adoptive parent grants her permission, or after she has lived with the child/ren for three years, or with leave of the court (Children Act 1989 s. 10). If the couple separate, the non-adoptive parent could apply for a contact order if necessary. (See also Chapter Seven.)

138   Valued Families

NOTES

1. The change in the number of children available for adoption is illustrated by the fact that in 1968, 25,000 children were adopted, over half of whom were less than one year old, but by 1991 the figure was only 7000. Half of these were children adopted by stepparents and other family members, and the number of babies adopted was less than 900 (White Paper 1993).

2. Case reference. Adoption Reports – Confidentiality 2. Fam. FLR 687.

3. Department of Health, *Family Placements*, vol 3 (1991).

4. Children can be privately adopted by a relative where they have lived continuously with her for at least 13 weeks. A relative is defined as a grandparent, sister, aunt, whether of full or half blood, or by affinity ('affinity' means a relationship through marriage).

CHAPTER 10

IMMIGRATION ISSUES

British immigration law is racist, sexist and heterosexist. People are treated differently and unequally, depending on whether they are British citizens, citizens of countries within the European Economic Area (EEA), or citizens of countries outside this area. They are also treated differently depending on their recognised marital status, which obviously can affect lesbian parents. This chapter looks at some aspects of the law that may affect lesbian parents, co-parents/partners and their children. Immigration law, however, is complicated and subject to frequent change. It is important therefore for lesbian parents to seek further information and advice from a specialist organisation or legal advice firm who are experts in the immigration field.

DEFINITIONS OF BASIC TERMS

What is 'immigration control'?

'Immigration control' means anything from a limit on the time someone is allowed to stay in the UK, and conditions on that stay – for example, having no recourse to public funds – to being refused entry completely. People can also be deported (sent out of the country) under certain circumstances, although in some cases there may be a right of appeal against deportation.

What is 'leave to remain'?

'Leave to remain' refers to the time and conditions that a person can stay in this country under immigration controls. Leave to remain can include a specific time-limited period, eg for one year, or can be specified as an indefinite period – indefinite leave to remain (also called 'settlement'; see below). People with leave to remain are still subject to immigration controls when they leave this country to go abroad and then return. In some cases if a person has been given only limited leave to remain, they may be refused re-entry if they leave the country and then try to return within that specified period.

What is 'settlement'?

'Settlement' refers to an immigration status in which the person has indefinite leave to remain in this country but is not a British citizen. People with settlement status are free to travel in and out of the country but are subject to immigration controls on re-entry, and they may be refused entry if they leave for more than two years. Even if they leave the UK for a short holiday, they still have to satisfy an immigration officer that they are residents in this country.

What is 'having no recourse to public funds'?

This is an immigration restriction that means that a person entering or living in the country cannot claim certain benefits. These include income support, family credit, housing benefit, council tax benefit and public housing. It does not include child benefit, free education, or national health service treatment.

What is 'citizenship'?

Having British citizenship gives the 'right of abode' – ie the right to live in the UK and come and go freely without immigration controls. As members of the European Union (EU), British citizens also have EU citizenship, as do the citizens of other member states. Each country within the EU has its own definitions of who qualifies for citizenship within that country.

LESBIAN PARENTS AND EU CITIZENSHIP

British immigration law is affected by Britain being a member of the EU. Britain and other member states, however, also have their own immigration regulations, which differ from state to state and can have different implications for lesbian parents.

EU citizenship and freedom of movement

EU law allows all people who hold EU citizenship to travel freely within the union to look for work, take up a job or become self-employed in a member state. EU citizens are also allowed to study or live in member countries if they have enough financial resources so that they will not become a burden on public funds. The only grounds on which freedom of movement can be curtailed by a member state are when 'public policy, public security and public health so require'.[1]

The countries that are full EU members at the time of writing are Austria, Belgium, Britain, Denmark, Finland, France, Germany, Greece, Ireland, Italy, Luxembourg, the Netherlands, Portugal, Spain and Sweden. EU freedom of movement rights are also extended to Norway and Iceland, and all these countries are now defined as being in the European Economic Area (EEA).

Lesbian parents' rights to be accompanied by their children

The principle of freedom of movement also allows EU citizens entering another member state for the purposes of work or study to be accompanied by their families. The family members who are allowed to accompany an EU citizen include dependent children and a spouse. Lesbian parents who are EU citizens can therefore move to live in Britain or another EU country with their dependent children. (In this case dependent children are defined as being under 21, or they can be over 21 if still dependent.)

Claiming benefits as EU citizens

It can be useful for an EU citizen to apply for a residence permit from the Home Office, as this may assist in demonstrating that she is 'habitually resident' in Britain if she needs to claim social security benefits sometime in the future. (Such a permit is not a compulsory requirement.) A lesbian mother who is working is entitled to claim family credit and to claim income support between jobs. If she comes to this country without a job and claims income support, however, the Home Office may be informed. She may be asked to leave if she cannot demonstrate that she is actively seeking work or has a genuine chance of finding employment, and further benefit may be refused.[2]

Partners/co-parents

A lesbian partner/co-parent is not recognised as a 'family member' in many EU countries, including Britain. A lesbian partner/co-parent who is an EU citizen has to show she is able to work or study in Britain in her own right before being allowed to live here on a long-term basis. If she is not an EU citizen she does not have the same legal rights to enter Britain and she is subject to a different set of immigration controls (see below).

Some EU countries do, however, recognise lesbian partners as 'family members' under their own immigration regulations, including partners who are not EU citizens. These countries include Denmark, Finland, the Netherlands, Norway and Sweden. This means it is possible for a lesbian parent who is an EU citizen to reside in one of the above countries with a long-term partner who is not an EU citizen, providing that they can meet the immigration regulations of that country.[3]

THE RIGHTS TO LIVE IN BRITAIN FOR LESBIAN PARENTS WHO ARE NOT EU CITIZENS

Dependency

A lesbian parent may have gained rights to live in Britain indefinitely if she has entered as a dependant through marriage.

Marriage to a British citizen

A lesbian mother who has been married to a British citizen and has remained living with her husband for at least twelve months without having recourse to public funds (the twelve-month rule) may be able to obtain indefinite leave to remain once the twelve months are up.

She should not have separated from her husband before the first twelve months of marriage, and when she applies for indefinite leave to remain the Home Office needs to be 'satisfied that the marriage has not ended' and that she and her spouse intend 'living permanently with each other as husband and wife'. She must have applied to the Home Office for leave to remain for one year in the first instance, on the grounds of her proposed marriage. In addition, an immigration officer must be satisfied that the marriage was genuine, ie that the marriage was not taking place merely so that the woman could live in Britain (the primary purpose rule).

If the woman has entered the country as a visitor, however, and then married without informing the Home Office of her change in circumstances, she could still be deported if she separates from her husband, even if one year has expired since the date of the marriage.

An application for indefinite leave to remain must be made after twelve months of marriage; it will not come into place automatically. Lesbian mothers should therefore not divorce or separate from their husbands until they have had 'indefinite leave to remain' stamped on their passports.

Women who are forced to leave a marriage before the twelve months are up – because of domestic violence, for example – could be deported if the Home Office becomes aware that they have left the marriage. They have no rights to claim income support or public housing on their own behalf. In rare cases a woman who is forced to leave a marriage because of violence may be granted exceptional leave to remain by the Home Office because of her particular circumstances, but this cannot be relied upon.

Marriage to an EU citizen

Where a woman is or has been married to an EU citizen her right to remain in this country is dependent on her husband's residence as an EU citizen. If she has been living here for four years with her husband and then separates, however, she may be able to get indefinite leave to remain on the basis of her long-term residence.

Marriage to students, work-permit holders and asylum seekers

The immigration status of a woman who has entered this country as the spouse of a non-EU student, work-permit holder or asylum seeker is entirely dependent on the immigration status of her husband. She has no right to stay if she separates from him or if his work permit or student status expire, or if he fails in his claim as an asylum seeker and is deported. Rarely she may be granted exceptional leave to remain, usually because of the effects of deportation on any children she may have. She should seek urgent legal advice on this matter.

Temporary entry to Britain

A lesbian parent who is not an EU citizen can enter Britain temporarily as a visitor, business visitor, working visitor, student or work-permit holder. However, visitors (including business visitors), prospective students and short-term students can be refused entry with no right of appeal under the Asylum and Immigration Appeals Act 1993. This Act was a racist measure introduced to deter black visitors to Britain, allowing junior immigration officers to refuse entry at their own discretion. Other immigration rules also exist which favour white Commonwealth citizens, since those who have a grandparent born in this country can apply for indefinite leave to remain on this basis, even if they have entered temporarily as a visitor. Those who enter Britain under a temporary status are usually not allowed to have recourse to public funds and must be self-supporting.

CHILDREN'S RIGHTS TO JOIN OR ACCOMPANY A PARENT WHO IS NOT AN EU CITIZEN

Children's immigration status in general depends on the immigration status of their parent.

A lesbian mother who is a lone parent must be able to show that she has sole responsibility for a child in order for the child to be able to accompany her or join her in Britain. This includes situations where she is applying for indefinite leave to remain (settlement) or she is already in the UK or planning to come to the UK as a student, work-permit holder or business visitor.

If, for example, she has had a child through donor insemination, she would need to be able to show she is the child's sole guardian. If she does not have sole responsibility, for example where she has been married and shares custody with the father, she needs to be able to show that the father is unable or unsuitable to care for the child and that the exclusion of the child from the mother is 'undesirable'. This rule is applied very stringently, but where a child is under 12 the Home Office has stated that he or she would 'fairly freely' be allowed to join a lone parent in the UK.[4] Lesbian parents in this situation are advised to check with a specialist organisation before making an application for their children to join them.

IMMIGRATION RULES AND LESBIAN PARTNERS

British immigration rules give no formal recognition to applications made for leave to remain on the basis of a same-sex relationship with a British citizen or someone settled here. However, the Home Office does have discretion to consider an application to remain here on this basis. In June 1996 the Stonewall Immigration Group reported that 17 partners had been given a year's leave to remain on the basis of a same-sex relationship. Out of these, three had been given indefinite leave to remain, and others were expected to follow. However, the report also stated that a large number of applications of equal merit had been refused.[5]

The factors that may be taken into account include

... the health of the settled partner and the length and stability of the relationship. An application will not be granted unless the relationship is long standing or there are other compelling compassionate features. Documentary evidence of the relationship, cohabitation and other relevant circumstances may be required.[6]

Each case is considered on its own merits, and there is no consistency in decisions made. However, the Home Office appears to regard a long-standing relationship as one of at least three years and in some cases over five years.[7]

In the case of lesbian parents making such an application, Stonewall has informed ROW that any parenting/co-parenting relationship with a child and the benefits of this relationship for the child should be stressed, as this can be taken into account as a factor when the application is considered by the Home Office. This applies where either partner is the biological parent of the child. Where it is the biological mother who does not have British citizenship, she will need to show that she has sole responsibility for her child (see above).

Lesbian parents considering making an application for leave to remain on the basis of a long-standing relationship are advised to seek information first from the Stonewall Immigration Group.

SEEKING ASYLUM

Seeking asylum and obtaining refugee status are now extremely difficult in any country in the EEA. These countries have combined to strengthen the 'Fortress Europe' concept by as much as possible restricting entry to asylum seekers.

The grounds for claiming refugee status and therefore being granted asylum are defined by the 1951 UN Convention on the Status of Refugees. The Convention requires that the applicant must demonstrate a 'well-founded fear of persecution for reasons of race, religion, nationality, membership of a particular social group, or political opinion' which prevents a person being able to return to their country of origin. There are no specific grounds relating to persecution either on the basis of gender or sexuality, but some countries (eg Canada) have recognised gender persecution as a basis for granting asylum, and others – including Australia, Canada, Denmark, Finland, Germany, the Netherlands, New Zealand and Sweden – have recognised that lesbians and gay men can constitute particular social groups under the grounds of the

UN Convention.[8] Britain, however, has so far given no such recognition.

Lesbian parents may claim asylum for other reasons if they feel their situation fits any of the categories mentioned above. However, unless they apply when they enter the country, they will not be able to claim any social security benefits or have access to public housing whilst they are waiting for their application to be heard.[9]

Exceptional leave to remain

The Home Office may decide not to grant full refugee status to asylum seekers, but may instead allow 'exceptional leave to remain/enter' initially for one year. Lesbian parents who do have full refugee status are entitled to have their children living with them. Those with exceptional leave to remain are subject to the same restrictions as temporary residents and would have to show that they have sole responsibility for any children before the children could join them.

ACQUIRING BRITISH CITIZENSHIP – IS IT WORTH IT?

It is possible to apply for British citizenship after living in this country for a number of years having fulfilled certain conditions, eg not having a criminal record. It is an extremely expensive and lengthy process, but it can have certain advantages, particularly in terms of freedom to travel abroad. However, applying for citizenship could jeopardise other kinds of immigration status, and it could mean losing citizenship of another country. It is therefore important to check with a specialist organisation before making an application.

CHILDREN AND BRITISH CITIZENSHIP

Anyone born in the UK or adopted in the UK before 1983 is a British citizen. After this date having British citizenship will depend on whether a child has a mother or (married) father who is a British citizen or who is settled in the UK. Children born to students or work-permit holders or to parents with exceptional leave to remain are not British citizens unless their parents have acquired settled status. But children born to EU nationals in Britain can be registered as British citizens.

NOTES

1. J Bhabha and S Shutter, *Women's Movement: Women under Immigration and Refugee Law*, Trentham Books, Staffs, 1994, p205.

2. S Shutter, *Immigration and Nationality Law Handbook*, Joint Council for the Welfare of Immigrants, London, 1995, p109.

3. Stonewall Immigration Group, 'United Kingdom Immigration Law and Rules as They Affect Same-Sex Couples', Stonewall, London, June 1996.

4. S Shutter, *Immigration and Nationality Law Handbook*.

5. Stonewall Immigration Group, 'United Kingdom Immigration Law and Rules as They Affect Same-Sex Couples', p4.

6. 'Letter to Stonewall Immigration Group from Neil Amos, private secretary to Immigration Minister, 19 April, 1995', Stonewall, London, 1996.

7. Stonewall Immigration Group, 'United Kingdom Immigration Law and Rules as They Affect Same-Sex Couples'.

8. Stonewall Immigration Group, 'United Kingdom Immigration Law and Rules as They Affect Same-Sex Couples', p13.

9. 1996 Asylum and Immigration Act.

CHAPTER 11

DOMESTIC VIOLENCE ISSUES

Domestic violence can involve the physical, sexual, and emotional abuse of women. The violence may be actual, threatened or attempted. In many cases where women are experiencing domestic violence the children may also be suffering abuse.[1]

Lesbian mothers coming out of a heterosexual relationship are often on the receiving end of domestic violence. The ending of the relationship may precipitate the violence, with some men being unable to accept that the relationship is over. Violence and/or intimidation may be used as an attempt to continue to control the mother and children. This may be used to prevent her from leaving, to try and force her to return to the relationship, or to take revenge. The violence may continue during the process of separation and after, for example when children are handed over for contact.[2]

HELP AND PROTECTION

No woman should have to put up with violence. This includes intimidation or the emotional undermining of herself or her mothering abilities. Research has also shown that domestic violence can seriously undermine the well-being of children who may witness or overhear the violence or intimidation of the mother.[3] Seeking help as soon as the abuse begins is an important first step, as once it starts it is rarely a one-off event.[4]

150

The law provides a limited amount of protection, and there are also a number of women's groups, refuges and agencies that can provide help (contact information is provided in Resources at the end of this book).

Lesbian mothers who are experiencing domestic violence may fear that if they do seek help and protection, they will lose their children. A father may threaten that if she takes him to court he will take the opportunity to seek residence of the children. In reality, lesbian mothers are unlikely to lose residence of their children because of their sexual identity.

Courts have the power to prevent a father having contact with children because of his violence towards their mother and/or them, particularly if it can be demonstrated that such violence is harming the children (Family Law Act 1996 s. 11, 42; Children Act 1989 s. 1). However, many judges continue to allow a violent father contact with the children, although in some cases this may be ordered to take place through a third party, or at a contact centre. There is an urgent need for a change of the law in this area so that there is an explicit legal presumption against contact where a partner has been violent.[5]

Domestic violence from a lesbian partner

There is widespread recognition that the vast majority of domestic violence is carried out by men.[6] In a few cases, however, women may abuse other women. Where a lesbian parent is experiencing threats or abuse from a lesbian partner or ex-partner, the legal protection discussed below also applies, unless otherwise specified. However, lesbians in this situation may need to act strategically and think carefully about using the law given the general level of anti-lesbianism prevalent amongst the police and in the legal system. For example, the police may be reluctant to act in a situation of domestic violence between lesbians, even where a serious assault has occurred. Lesbians experiencing domestic violence from a lesbian partner may want to seek legal advice from ROW or a lesbian organisation before taking action.

PROTECTION UNDER THE CRIMINAL LAW

The law regards an assault which takes place within the home as a crime. This now includes rape within marriage. However, when a crime or incident is reported to the police, they have discretion on what action to take. In 1990, as a result of years of pressure from women's organisations, a Home Office circular (60/1990) stressed that violence in the home is 'no less serious than a violent assault by a stranger'. It stated that police forces should stop decriminalising domestic violence. In consequence, police practices have changed, although they may still vary in different parts of the country.[7]

The police have the power to arrest a perpetrator (someone who has committed a criminal offence) and remove him from the scene when a domestic assault has taken place. They also have the power of arrest to protect vulnerable persons where they have reason to believe an assault or other crime is imminent (Police and Criminal Evidence Act 1984). A number of police stations have set up domestic violence units to advise women on what action they can take.

In situations where a lesbian mother and/or her children are being threatened with, or are experiencing, immediate physical or sexual violence, the police should be called and the woman can insist that the perpetrator is arrested. However, taking such action will usually only afford her short-term protection. The man may be held overnight and released without charge, or released after only a few hours. In some cases the police may merely issue an official warning. Even if he is charged and comes before a court, he may only be fined or released with conditions rather than sent to prison. This depends on the nature and seriousness of the offence.[8]

If a woman is not able to call the police at the time, she can phone or call in at a police station and make an appointment to speak to an officer from the domestic violence unit (where there is one) and get advice about what action should be taken.

Where a woman has experienced physical injury or rape, she can be examined by a police doctor to provide evidence of such injury. However, she herself may have to give evidence and she may be asked by the police whether she wishes to pursue her complaint and give evidence against the perpetrator. If she states that she does not wish to do so, the police can decide not to charge him, or charges already brought may be dropped by the Crown Prosecution Service (CPS) who take the case to court. Alternatively, a woman can be compelled by the CPS to give evidence in court.

Deciding what action to take will very much depend on the circumstances and whether the woman believes that charging the perpetrator will have a deterrent effect. The failure of the courts to send men to prison in cases of domestic violence, except in repeated cases or where there is evidence of serious injury, can also place her and her children in continued jeopardy.

Currently the benefits of using the police and the criminal law lie mainly in removing the perpetrator from the scene. This can give a woman some respite so that she can escape with her children to a place of safety. In these situations, the police should also provide assistance. Police involvement can also be useful in providing evidence to a court of a father's unsuitability to have residence or contact with the children, or in an application for a civil order for protection (see below).

Racism and the police

It has to be recognised that because of racism in a number of police forces they may be slower to act in domestic violence situations involving black women and men.[9] Alternatively, black men who are arrested may be treated far more severely by the police than white men. In addition, the insecure immigration status of some women may make it difficult for them to call the police, in case their immigration status is called into question. In these situations the criminal law offers little or no protection.

PROTECTION UNDER THE CIVIL LAW

Non-molestation and occupation orders

Part IV of the Family Law Act 1996 (FLA) has simplified the remedies for protection from domestic violence and broadened the categories of people who can apply for them. The provisions of this Act which relate to obtaining protection from domestic violence are due to come into force in October 1997.

The Act has replaced the old types of injunctions which could be obtained previously and introduced two types of orders that can be used in situations of domestic violence or abuse of children: non-molestation orders and occupation orders. Before the Act, orders for protection were sometimes called injunctions. It will still be necessary to apply for injunctions if people do not fall within the provisions of the Act as explained below. In these circumstances, women should seek advice from Rights of Women, a solicitor or advice centre. Whatever the order is called, it can instruct a violent man not to harass or assault a woman and/or children and can sometimes order him to leave the home. It is a written document given to a man. If he disobeys it, he can be fined or sent to prison.

For married women who are experiencing domestic violence and are applying for a divorce, the existence of a Part IV order is good evidence of the need for a shorter 'reflection and consideration' period (see Chapter Six). If a woman has obtained an occupation or non-molestation order, her divorce can be granted in 12 rather than 18 months. Until January 1999 when the FLA divorce provisions are due to be implemented, a woman can usually obtain a divorce within 7–9 months in cases of domestic violence.

A non-molestation order prohibits particular behaviour and/or general molestation of the applicant and/or her children. It is made against a person who is 'associated' (as defined within the Act) with the woman or her child (FLA 1996 s. 42). A child is also able to apply for a non-molestation order if she or he obtains leave of the court.

In its definition of 'associated persons', ie people against whom an order can be made, the Act includes: people who are or have been married or have agreed to marry; people who are or have been living in a cohabiting relationship (heterosexual); and people who are or have been living in the same household but are not merely employees, tenants or lodgers. It also includes relatives and people who are parents of, or have parental responsibility for, a child (FLA 1996 s. 62). A current or former lesbian live-in partner would therefore be regarded as an 'associated person' under the category of 'people who are or have been living in the same household'. She would not fall into the category of 'cohabitant', however.

An occupation order excludes a violent person from the family home and surrounding area and gives the applicant and her child(ren) rights to occupy the home (FLA 1996 s. 33). However, there are various issues that a court has to consider before making such an order. These are:

- the housing needs and housing resources of each of the parties and of any relevant child;

- the financial resources of each of the parties;

- the likely effect of any order or decision by the court on the health, safety or well-being of the parties and of any relevant child;

- the conduct of the parties in relation to each other and otherwise; and

- whether the applicant or relevant child is likely to suffer significant harm from the conduct of the respondent (the person against whom the order is made) if an order is not made.

To confuse the issue even further the court also has to consider the 'significant harm' to the respondent (the violent party!) and to a relevant child if an order is made.

It is clear from the Parliamentary debates on this issue

when the Family Law Bill was being discussed that there was a strong lobby aimed at protecting the interests of violent fathers. Some of the matters to be considered in making orders relate to the concern of these groups. It is not yet certain how the factors listed above will be interpreted by the courts, as the Act has not yet come into effect.

The fourth clause above, relating to the conduct of the parties, may be taken to mean that a court should give full consideration to the violent behaviour of one party. However, it could be interpreted negatively for lesbian mothers if a judge is aware that a woman has left a heterosexual relationship/marriage for a lesbian one. This is one of the issues which may be the subject of appeal and caselaw.

Occupation orders for married women

A woman who is married can obtain an occupation order even if she has no financial interest in the home or her name is not on the tenancy. Tenancy rights can be transferred to her name. If she is divorced she may still be able to apply for an order depending on the circumstances. Occupation orders granted to married women can be for a specified period, or run indefinitely until another order is made.

Occupation orders for cohabitants

A cohabitant (defined in the Act as a woman and man living together as husband and wife) or former cohabitant has less right to obtain an occupation or transfer of tenancy order than a married woman if she has no financial interest in the home or her name is not on the tenancy. In this case the court also has to consider how long she has been living with the respondent and how long (in the case of former cohabitants) since she stopped living with him, before making an order. The maximum total period for which she can obtain an occupation order is only one year.

This blatant discrimination between cohabitants/former cohabitants and married women is the result of the 'family values' lobby attempting to establish the supremacy of legal marriage over all other forms of relationship. Despite strong lobbying during the passage of the FLA through Parliament, all attempts to place married and unmarried women on the same legal footing in terms of protection from violence and abuse failed. This unjustifiable discrimination is clearly enshrined in section 41 (2) of the Act, which instructs that 'the court ... is to have regard to the fact that they [the parties to the case] have not given each other the commitment involved in marriage'.

Occupation orders and lesbians living together
A lesbian mother sharing a home with a partner can also apply for an occupation order against a violent lesbian partner if she has a financial interest in the property or her name is on the tenancy (FLA 1996 s. 33 (1) (a)). Otherwise she cannot apply for an occupation order in such circumstances.

Powers of arrest

One of the positive aspects of the FLA is that it has strengthened a court's position to attach a power of arrest (POA) to occupation orders and non-molestation orders (FLA 1996 s. 47). Powers of arrest enable a police officer to arrest a respondent where she/he 'has reasonable cause for suspecting' an order has been breached and to bring him before a court within 24 hours. Once the violent partner has been brought before a court, the court has the power to commit him to prison for breach of the order.

Currently POAs are infrequently attached to injunctions and usually only in cases of extreme violence. Under the FLA a POA *must* be attached to an order where the respondent has used or threatened violence against an applicant or a relevant child, unless it appears that adequate protection is available without such a power. Under the old rules, in order to have a POA attached to an order, injuries classifiable at least as actual bodily harm must have occurred and there had to be a strong likelihood of it happening again. However, in practice, judges were reluctant to attach a POA even when actual bodily harm had clearly been demonstrated.

Undertakings

The courts have the power not to make an order at all but
to accept an undertaking from the respondent. An undertaking is a promise to the court by the respondent not to
molest the applicant, or a promise to leave or stay away
from the family home. A POA cannot be attached to an
undertaking. However, the Act states that an undertaking
should not be accepted by the court where a POA would
be attached if an order were made (FLA 1996 s. 46 (3)).
Undertakings are frequently breached by violent men and
cannot be relied upon to protect women and children.

Ex-parte orders

An ex-parte order is one which is made where the respondent
(here the violent partner) has not been given notice of the
proceedings and is therefore not in court. Ex-parte orders
are usually made when it is necessary to provide immediate
protection for a woman and/or child or where the violent
partner may be evading having notice of the proceedings
served on him.

Third-party applications

The Act also makes it possible for a third party to apply for
a non-molestation order or occupation order on behalf of a
victim of domestic violence (FLA s. 60). Such a situation
could apply where a victim is unwilling or unable to make
an application herself but is prepared for someone else to act
on her behalf. The Act does not specify who can make such
applications, but provides for rules to be laid down in this
respect. At present it would appear likely that the police
or the Women's Aid Federation would be the most likely
organisations to apply for an order on behalf of a victim of
violence.

Specific protection of children from child abuse

The Act now makes it possible for an abuser to be removed from the home under an emergency care order. These orders can be obtained by a local authority exercising its powers to protect children. It is useful to have an order to remove the abuser rather than take the child out of the home for his or her benefit, as happens often at present. The abuser can usually be removed for as long as the emergency care order is in force, if the child is still living in the home. The order for removal may be made if the court is satisfied of the risk of harm to the child. But the mother or other carer for the child must agree that the order should be made.

OBTAINING REFUGE AND HOUSING

In some situations neither the criminal nor the civil law provides adequate protection from violent men. In such cases women have to escape from the family home. Where a woman has to flee because of violence, she should, where possible, always take her children with her. (If the children are already living with her and she needs to seek a residence order later, she will stand a better chance of keeping the children.) If she has to leave the children she should try and keep contact with them, eg by phone or letter (see Chapter Six).

The Women's Aid Federation (England) provides a network of refuges throughout the country for women and children leaving violent men, as well as giving advice to women experiencing domestic violence (a contact number is given in Resources at the back of this book). Refuges are safe spaces run by and for women, which provide emergency accommodation for women who have had to leave home to escape violence but who have nowhere else to go, or who are afraid that their partner will find them if they stay with relatives or friends. There are also refuges which cater particularly to the needs of Asian and African-Caribbean women and which can provide a safe, non-racist environment for black women, and a very few refuges for disabled women.

There are not nearly enough refuges to cater for all the women who need them, and whether there is a place available when needed depends on local circumstances. Refuges can usually provide help and advice in claiming benefits, and many have childcare workers on site. Additionally, they usually have links with local solicitors who are experienced in domestic violence issues.

Local authorities have certain duties to women with children who are made homeless as a result of domestic violence (Housing Act 1996, Parts VI and VII). These duties are less extensive than under the previous legislation. But in general, local authorities are still initially required to ensure that temporary accommodation is available for the woman and children. This is often in cramped bed-and-breakfast hostels. However, even this type of accommodation can provide a welcome respite free of violence and can be challenged if totally unsuitable. Unfortunately, once a woman and children have been housed for two years the local authority may no longer be under any duties towards them. This may result in women and children who have been made homeless because of domestic violence having to reapply again as homeless after the initial two-year period.

However, women with children must still be given reasonable preference in secure housing allocation. Immigration status may be a bar to obtaining either temporary or permanent housing assistance, and legal advice should be sought immediately in this situation. For details of occupation or transfer of tenancy orders which may sometimes be obtained for a woman, see 'Non-molestation and occupation orders' above.

CHILD CONTACT WITH VIOLENT MEN

Many women who have experienced domestic violence do not wish the father to have any contact with the children. Children may themselves have been abused, and contact frequently puts a woman's safety at risk. However, courts continue to regard contact with the father as in the children's best interests, even where he has been abusive in the past. Contact orders are sometimes made at the same time as a woman applies for an injunction. Assumptions of contact in these circumstances should be challenged. A woman who feels that contact would be against the children's welfare or would threaten her own health or capability to care for the children should advise her lawyer accordingly. Being able to produce material evidence in court – such as medical evidence of abuse, police reports, doctors' letters, letters from the children's schools, child guidance services and in some cases social services reports – will help to demonstrate to the court that contact is not in the children's best interests (see also Chapter Six).

Where a court makes a contact order, a woman should insist that contact is arranged through a third party or takes place at a contact centre (although very few of these exist) so that her own safety and/or that of her children is not put at risk. She should also ensure that her address is not revealed.

MEDIATION

The Family Law Act 1996 places great emphasis on the use of mediation to settle disputes following marriage breakdown. However, mediation is usually recognised to be inappropriate in situations of domestic violence. The power imbalance as a result of an abusive relationship could result in a negative outcome for the woman in mediation. In addition, women have been attacked going to and from mediation meetings and in the meetings themselves.[10] However, the Act does state that where a divorce is being sought, a court may give a direction requiring each party to attend a meeting for the purposes of being given information about mediation. It also states that the parties must attend the same meeting 'unless one or both of them ask for separate meetings' (FLA 1996 s. 13). Women who are experiencing domestic violence should request a separate meeting and inform the mediator that mediation is inappropriate for them because they fear for their own safety.

CHILD SUPPORT

Where a woman is in receipt of income support, family credit or disability working allowance, she is expected to cooperate with the Child Support Agency (CSA) in enabling them to pursue the biological father for maintenance. If she does not cooperate with the CSA she can be penalised by a benefit reduction. The Child Support Act 1991 does recognise, however, that in situations where women fear harm to themselves or their children they may have good cause not to cooperate (CSA 1991 s. 6(2)). In these circumstances, a woman will usually be called to an interview to give her reasons. Where possible she should take someone with her to witness the interview. There is increasing anecdotal evidence that CSA staff are demanding proof that a woman or child has been abused before they will accept her reasons for non-cooperation, although this is contrary to CSA guidelines. However, documentary proof will always assist a woman to convince the CSA that she falls within the exemption. For example, medical or police reports, as well as copies of court orders, are likely to be helpful.

A woman can also appeal against a CSA decision to reduce her benefit because her reasons for non-cooperation have not been accepted.

GETTING ADVICE AND SUPPORT

Women who are experiencing domestic violence need to obtain good legal advice and support. Where a woman is also seeking a residence and/or contact order, she needs to find a solicitor who is able to advise on these issues as well. Contact information is provided in Resources at the back of this book.

NOTES

1. Marianne Hester and Lorraine Radford, *Domestic Violence and Child Contact Arrangements in England and Denmark*, Policy Press, Bristol, 1996.

2. Marianne Hester and Lorraine Radford, *Domestic Violence and Child Contact Arrangements in England and Denmark*.

3. Audrey Mullender and Rebecca Morley, eds, *Children Living with Domestic Violence: Putting Men's Abuse of Women on the Childcare Agenda*, Whiting and Birch, London, 1994.

4. WAFE Information Pack, Women's Aid Federation England, Bristol, 1991.

5. Marianne Hester and Lorraine Radford, *Domestic Violence and Child Contact Arrangements in England and Denmark*.

6. Home Affairs Committee, Domestic Violence (1992–3) Third Report HC 245.

7. WAFE Information Pack.

8. WAFE Information Pack.

9. Jill Radford, 'Policing Male Violence – Policing Women', in J Hammer and M Maynard, eds, *Women, Violence and Social Control*, Macmillan, London, 1985; Southall Black Sisters, 'Domestic Violence and Asian Women. A Collection of Reports and Briefings', Southall Black Sisters, London, 1993.

10. Marianne Hester and Lorraine Radford, *Domestic Violence and Child Contact Arrangements in England and Denmark*.

CHAPTER 12

LIVING AS LESBIAN PARENTS

Lesbian parenting is a positive choice. The many happy children who have grown up in lesbian households are living proof of that, but discrimination still exists within some institutions such as schools and the health-care system. This chapter discusses the benefits and pitfalls of lesbian parenting in a generally heterosexual community.

Whilst acceptance of lesbian families is becoming more widespread, in some cases prejudice can be compounded by racism and discriminatory practices towards women with disabilities, as is reflected by the following statements:

> Being closeted is not a choice I wish to make. Nevertheless, because of the pervasiveness of racism it is one I choose to make. Terri and I are fully aware that as Black lesbians, raising children in a white, racist, sexist and homophobic society, we are fighting a system that threatens to devour us and our children.[1]

> I am constantly having to deal with the message from the whole world that I couldn't possibly be a good parent because of my disabilities. It's funny no one seems to be worried that I am a lesbian; they are completely fixated on my being disabled.[2]

This chapter discusses a few aspects of living as a lesbian parent, in particular health matters and education.

HEALTH MATTERS

Choosing a doctor

It is very important to choose a general practitioner (GP) who can offer you the kind of services you may need. Your local Health Authority, or Health Board in Scotland and Northern Ireland, and/or your local Community Health Council can provide a list of GPs in your area and advice and information about the services they offer. In addition, local community groups and telephone helplines may be able to suggest doctors who are appropriate for you (see Resources).

When you approach a general practice surgery, ask for their practice leaflet, which should describe how the practice is run, the staff working there and the services offered. Some issues you may want to consider in selecting a practice are when clinics are held, whether there is an appointment or open-door system and whether there are any women doctors and nurses practising in the surgery.

Confidentiality

If you come out as a lesbian to your doctor and do not want your sexuality disclosed, bear in mind that doctors are not legally obliged to respect your wishes within the health service. However, anybody wanting information on your medical background, for example an employer, must ask your permission before approaching your doctor.

Maternity services

Maternity care can be provided by a midwife, a GP, a hospital consultant and her or his team or, more usually, by a combination of all three. If you are already registered with a GP, you can register with another for antenatal and delivery care, while remaining with the first GP for all other health care. If you are not registered with a GP you will not be refused care at a hospital during pregnancy. You may, however, choose to have maternity care provided by an independent or NHS midwife.

You have several options about place of birth. You may choose to give birth in hospital as an admission, in a special GP or Domino Unit in hospital, or at home. All pregnant women have the right to receive care from a midwife during pregnancy and birth. Following the birth you will receive home visits from community midwives until ten days after delivery, or longer if there are any problems. A health visitor will then visit and provide support and information.

For information on maternity rights, see Appendix C.

Health advice

For friendly and detailed advice on any health-related issue, call Women's Health, who operate a free telephone advice service (see Resources for details). Women's Health also runs a self-insemination group and produces publications on a whole range of health issues including lesbian health, fertility and general health issues.

For information on any NHS service you can contact the free national Health Information Service (see Resources).

CHILD CARE

Information on lesbian-friendly childminders and playgroups might be found in the *Pink Paper* or by contacting the local switchboard or lesbian and gay phone line for your area.

Lesbian mothers could also place their own advertisements – in the *Pink Paper*, for example – to set up an informal child-care arrangement or play scheme.

EDUCATION

Despite Clause 28 (see Chapter One), which stated that local authorities must not promote homosexuality as a 'pretended family relationship', many nursery and primary schools are generally accepting of children of lesbians. Many, even in small towns, will accept that a child has two mothers and will write down both names as contacts in an emergency. Most are also prepared to accept that both mothers may attend parents' evenings. A few individual schools are pre-pared to go further than this and provide books that feature children having two mothers (some of these are listed in Resources at the end of this book).

Some primary schools also have equal opportunities poli-cies which allow teachers to address the issue of children growing up in 'different' families, but many are fairly con-servative in this area. For example, one mother pointed out that on 'Mother's Day' and 'Father's Day', schools generally tend to be insensitive to the fact that a child has two mothers or that she/he has no father when the children are asked to make cards to take home.

Another lesbian mother stated that at her children's primary school the teachers had been fine about their situ-ation until one of her children was having difficulties at school. It was then suggested that it might have been better if the child had only one mother.

Secondary and special schools may be more conservative than primary and nursery schools, although this is not always the case. One woman visited the headteachers of three sec-ondary schools in a provincial city and asked them what they could offer children of lesbians. Whilst one head said 'nothing', a second thought he would need to provide some books, and the third stated that it would be a positive advantage to have the children of a lesbian in the school and he would talk to them about their needs.

Speaking positively about the inner London school she attended, a 14-year-old girl said she had faced no problems because the school had an equal opportunities policy and it did not allow teasing or bullying of children from 'different types of families'. She was therefore able to be totally open about her family situation. Alternatively, a boy who attended a secondary school for children with special needs and had been born through self-insemination said that his teachers refused to accept that he did not have a father.

Attitudes of other children can vary. It is obviously up to the child themselves what they tell their friends at school, but they need to be aware of their peer group's attitudes and how their families can be perceived as different (see also Chapter Two).

Lesbian mothers can affect the policies and practices of schools in a positive way by volunteering for school governing bodies. Governing bodies have responsibility for formulating school policies including equal opportunities statements, and some lesbian mothers have been able to bring about dynamic changes in their child's school by becoming a governor.

Inevitably, coping with social prejudice can seem difficult at times, but within lesbian families, both mothers and children often name it as an ultimately positive experience. One mother described in an interview for this book how her teenage sons have developed greater awareness:

> They have an understanding of how discrimination against people operates, in particular of sexism and heterosexism and other oppressions such as racism and discrimination against people with disabilities. They are more respectful of women and they have a greater depth of understanding of the society in which they live.

Also in an interview for this book, a 14-year-old girl described the changes she sees in herself:

> I have a wider, more open view about other people and

their differences. I feel I am more tolerant towards people who experience prejudice and discrimination for other reasons. I am also more aware of the choices I have and can make when I am grown up.

GETTING SUPPORT

Whatever a woman's specific situation, finding support, particularly from other lesbian mothers, can help both in dealing with discrimination and prejudice and sharing the good times. Many children have also said how they have benefited from knowing the children of other lesbians:

Knowing other children of lesbian mothers has been quite important for me. I think that if I hadn't had it I would have felt quite isolated and lonely, shrunk inside myself and all on my own, but because I did have it, I don't feel bad.[3]

I think its quite important to know other children of lesbians. I need to chat with someone else about it. I need to know I am not the only person in the world like this. Sheila [his mother] has started up a lesbian mothers' and children's network. That's great. I feel more relaxed with those people because they will understand.[4]

A number of networks for lesbian mothers and their children exist in the larger cities throughout the country. There may also be groups which exist specifically for black and/or Asian lesbians. They can usually be contacted via the local lesbian line phone number, often now listed in Thompson's Directory or the Yellow Pages. See also Resources at the back of this book.

170   Valued Families

NOTES

1. Akanke, 'Black in the Closet', in D Epstein, ed, *Challenging Lesbian and Gay Inequalities in Education*, Open University Press, Buckingham, 1994.

2. Quoted in C Pies, *Considering Parenthood*, Spinsters Book Company, San Francisco, 1988.

3. Jenny, age 12 in 1992, quoted in Lisa Saffron, *Challenging Conceptions: Planning a Family by Self-Insemination*, Cassell, London, 1994.

4. Tim, age 12 in 1992, quoted in Lisa Saffron, *Challenging Conceptions: Planning a Family by Self-Insemination*.

Appendices

LESBIANS HAVING CHILDREN TOGETHER

Where there is no biological father involved in the upbringing of the child, the issue for a lesbian mother who has a partner is 'Do I want my partner to be involved in the upbringing of my child?' and, if so, 'Do I want to share the legal responsibilities with her?'

If the answer to both questions is 'yes', then an application can be made for joint residence. Any person who has a residence order made in her favour will also automatically have parental responsibility (PR).

PARENTAL RESPONSIBILITY

The biological mother of a child will automatically have parental responsibility (PR). If she is married at the time of the birth the husband will also automatically have PR. An unmarried father can obtain PR by agreement with the mother or by court order. Any other individual can only obtain PR if a residence order is made in her or his favour. For women who have agreed to have a child together it is important for the non-biological mother to obtain PR, to give her rights to make day-to-day decisions in the child's life, for example, in relation to the child's health (such as agreeing to vaccinations and operations and receiving the results of tests) and schooling and to simplify taking the child abroad on holiday.

APPLICATIONS FOR RESIDENCE

Usually the non-biological mother will make the application. She is therefore the Applicant.

If the biological mother agrees to the making of the order and there is no one else with PR, the procedure is relatively straightforward. What follows is the result of experience gained in a number of cases. It is important to remember that because this is a relatively new area of law, the procedure can vary from area to area and from judge to judge.

LEGAL AID

It may be difficult to obtain legal aid – in a recent case legal aid was refused precisely because this type of application was so straightforward. The parties were in agreement and the courts, it was said, were making such orders every day. Women who are not eligible for legal aid may not wish to use solicitors because of the cost, or women may simply wish to make the application themselves.

THE BIOLOGICAL MOTHER

By agreeing to a joint residence order a biological mother is agreeing to diminish some of her own rights, because she will be sharing PR. It is important that she considers this. Any order made now could have implications in the future if the relationship breaks down and there are contested proceedings in relation to the child.

If the biological mother is aware of the effects of the order and agrees to them, it is a good idea for her to complete the Answer to the Application Form, so that the court has a record that she is in agreement. Some biological mothers may wish to visit a solicitor (separate from the Applicant's solicitor if she has one) and obtain a letter which indicates that the solicitor has explained to her that by agreeing to the making of the order she is diminishing her own rights.

THE DONOR

When the child has been born by artificial insemination using a known donor, some courts have indicated a wish to have documentary evidence from the father that he wants no part in the child's life and agrees to the making of an order in favour of the co-parent. Strictly speaking this is not necessary if the man does not have PR. Nonetheless this is a possibility to be aware of and if such evidence is asked for, the Applicant could ask the donor to write a letter to that effect.

It may be that the father plays a part in the child's life but is agreeable to the making of the order. If the father is involved at all the judge may wish to hear from him about this, either by letter or by evidence in person.

It is always important to bear in mind the implications of revealing the identity of the biological father to the court. This could be detrimental for the man (resulting in possible problems with the Child Support Agency) and for the mother (if at a later stage the man wishes to assert his parental rights).

It is important to bear in mind that *any* public acknowledgement by the mothers or the donor of his identity may in the future bring him and them into conflict with the Child Support Agency.

LEAVE TO MAKE AN APPLICATION FOR A RESIDENCE ORDER

If the biological mother agrees to the making of the order (and there is no one else who has PR), there will be no need to apply for leave to make an application for a residence order. If the matter is not agreed, leave to make the application is required from the court, unless the non-biological mother, the Applicant, has lived with the child for more than three years, ending not more than three months ago. If the biological mother, or anyone else, objects to the making of the order, the court will consider the nature of the proposed application, the Applicant's connection with the child and any risk that the application might disrupt the child's life. If there is an objection, particularly from the biological mother, legal advice should be sought.

THE APPLICATION FORM

The Applicant completes the C1 Application for an Order (Children Act 1989). (See pro forma at pp181–4.) The form can be obtained from law stationers (eg Oyez, 144 Fetter Lane, London EC4, 0171 405 2847, for £1 each) or from local magistrates' or county courts or the Principal Registry of the Family Division at Somerset House in the Strand in London.

How the form is filled in is very important. If the biological mother has more than one child for whom a residence order is required, all their names should be entered on one form. If both partners have children and want orders, each woman should complete a form in relation to her own child or children.

The form is self-explanatory, but there are certain matters that should be made clear.

Section 1 About you. The Applicant, the non-biological mother, should indicate that she has had a major role in the care and upbringing of the child since birth (or whenever). Leave the solicitor's details blank if you are representing yourself.

Section 2 The child(ren) and the order(s) you are applying for. After giving the name, sex, age and address of the child, the Applicant should state that she is applying for a joint residence order with the biological mother.

Section 3 Other cases which concern the child(ren). If there have ever been any other court proceedings about the children in this application, details of those cases should be entered here.

Section 4 The Respondent(s). In this case the biological

mother will be the Respondent. The father will only be a Respondent if he has obtained PR. If he has PR he should be informed of the application. He could object to the making of a joint residence order.

Section 5   **Others to whom notice is to be given.** If the child is being accommodated by the local authority, the local authority should be informed of the application. If there are other people who are caring for the child when the application is made, they should be informed. Anyone whose name appears on any other court order which concerns the child and which is still in effect should be informed; anyone in other proceedings concerning the child which are about to commence should be informed, unless the Applicant believes that that order or those proceedings are irrelevant. Anyone with whom the child has lived for at least three years prior to the application should be informed. In practice this section will probably not be applicable and should therefore be left blank.

Section 6   **The care of the child(ren).** Indicate here who the child lives with and the shared care given by both mothers. If there are other children living in the home, give their details (name and age) and state how close the children are – for example, that they treat each other like brothers and sisters.

Section 7   **Social Services.** This is only relevant if the child has had any contact with Social Services.

Section 8   **The education and health of the child(ren).** If the child is at school and/or has any particular health problems, this should be described here.

Section 9   **The parent(s) of the child(ren).** Here include the fact that the Respondent is the mother and then describe the role of the father:
  • If the child was conceived through a clinic registered under the terms of the Human Fertilisation and Embry-

ology Act 1990, this should be stated. There will then
be no further question as to the donor.

- If the child was not conceived through a clinic the court
will possibly show more interest in the donor's position.
It may be that the man was a donor who is unknown
to the Applicant, in which case state this. He may be a
man who is known to the Applicant but who donated
sperm for the sole purpose of assisting the biological
mother to become pregnant, knowing that the intention
was for the Applicant and the biological mother (the
Respondent) to have a child and that he would play no
part in the child's life. If that is so, make that point and
if possible expand on it by indicating that the man has
never seen the child, maintained the child, has no contact
with the child and that his address is now unknown
(include any or all of these, but only if they are
appropriate).

- If the donor has been involved in the child's life or the
Applicant would like him to become involved, this may
be indicated. If so the Applicant or the donor may be
written to by the court and asked for more details, and
he may be required to attend the hearing (even though
he is not a party because he does not have parental
responsibility).

Section 10   The family of the child(ren) (other children). If
there are other children who are not currently living with
the Applicant but who have a biological relationship with the
child in question, state their details: name, address, age, and
their relationship, if any, with the child in the case.

Section 11   Other adults. This section refers to other adults
who may live at the same address as the child. Their details
should be included here.

Section 12   Your reason(s) for applying and any plans for
the child(ren). In this section indicate the reasons for applying
that have been mentioned above, to do with the child's health,
education, holidays, the importance for other children in the

family that all members of the family are legally connected with each other and any other reasons which relate to the child's welfare. If these reasons are stated clearly and succinctly they should fit into the space provided; alternatively, indicate that the answer to this question continues on another sheet of paper. This way there will be no need to make a separate statement, which will save costs and time.

The form is not intended for extended statements, but statements setting out the history of the case can be prepared and taken to the first hearing in order to save time.

Section 13   **At the court**. Indicate here if an interpreter will be attending court (and if so, specify the language required), or if facilities for the disabled will be required.

THE COURT

The Applicant can choose in which court to lodge the application form, usually the Magistrates' Court or the County Court. The matter will probably be dealt with most efficiently by the County Court. Indicate to the court staff that the matter is agreed. The effect of this is that there is no need for a hearing to make an application for leave. Tell them that a conciliation appointment is not necessary. What is needed is simply a directions hearing (before a district judge if the matter is dealt with in the County Court). Say that the hearing should take no more than thirty minutes.

THE HEARING

Both parties should attend the hearing. The children do not need to attend. The hearing will probably be in a small room with a fairly informal atmosphere.

The Applicant speaks first and should introduce herself and the Respondent to the judge and give the name(s) and age(s) of the child(ren). If the parents are unrepresented, the judge will probably ask questions to help.

The judge will need to know from the Applicant:

- why she is making the application,
- that the biological mother is in agreement,
- that the biological mother realises that the granting of a residence order to the non-biological mother means that the biological mother loses her absolute PR, and
- the position of the donor – this will usually be that he does not have PR and that there has never been and will never be any involvement by him in the child's life, either because he donated sperm through a clinic or because of the particular agreement between him and the parties about his role.

After the Applicant has spoken the Respondent speaks, covering the same issues. The judge will ask a few more questions and then make the order.

This is only an outline of the way a hearing may proceed. Some judges try to make the procedure extremely informal, and ask questions of both parties, in no particular order. The main thing is to ensure that the judge has all the relevant facts and that s/he knows that these orders are now being made all the time (see *Re C* (a minor) residence order: lesbian co-parents, 24 June 1994, a decision of Douglas Brown J, a High Court Judge, reported in (1994) *Fam Law* 468).

If the Applicant is unrepresented and the judge or magistrate seems to find difficulty with making the order for joint residence, it may be wise to ask for an adjournment to obtain legal advice. The ROW advice line can help with this (see Resources).

Application for an Order   Form C1
(Children Act 1989)

	To be completed by the Court
The Court	
	Date issued
The full name(s) of the child(ren)	
	Case number
	Child(ren)'s number(s)

1. About you (the Applicant).

State

- your title, full name, address, telephone number, date of birth and relationship to each child above
- your solicitor's name, address, reference, telephone, fax and DX numbers.

2. The child(ren) and the order(s) you are applying for.

For each child state

- the full name, date of birth and sex
- the type of order(s) you are applying for (for example, residence order, contact order, supervision order).

3.   Other cases which concern the child(ren).

If there have ever been, or there are pending, any court cases which concern
  - a child whose name you have put in paragraph 2
  - a full, half or step brother or sister of a child whose name you have put in paragraph 2
  - a person in this case who is or has been, involved in caring for a child whose name you have put in paragraph 2.

please attach a copy of the relevant order and give
  - the name of the Court
  - the name and panel address (if known) of the guardian ad litem, if appointed
  - the name and contact address (if known) of the court welfare officer, if appointed
  - the name and contact address (if known) of the solicitor appointed for the child(ren).

4.   The Respondent(s).

(Appendix 3 Family Proceedings Courts Rules 1991; Schedule 2 Family Proceedings (Children Act 1989) Rules 1991).

For each Respondent state
  - the title, full name and address
  - the date of birth (if known) or the age
  - the type relationship to each child.

5.   Others to whom notice is to be given.

(Appendix 3 Family Proceedings Rules 1991; Schedule 2 Family Proceedings Courts (Children Act 1989) Rules 1991)

For each person state
  - the title, full name and address
  - the date of birth (if known) or age
  - the relationship to each child.

6. The care of the child(ren).

For each child in paragraph 2 state
- the child's current address and how long the child has lived there
- whether it is the child's usual address and who cares for the child there
- the child's relationship to the other children (if any).

7. Social Services.

For each child in paragraph 2 state
- whether the child is known to the Social Services. If so, give the name of the social worker and the address of the Social Services Department
- whether the child is, or has been, on the Child Protection Register. If so, give the date of registration.

8. The education and health of the child(ren).

For each child state
- the name of the school, college or place of training which the child attends
- whether the child is in good health. Give details of any serious disabilities or ill health
- whether the child has any special needs.

9. The Parent(s) of the child(ren).

For each child state
- the full name of the child's mother and father
- whether the parents are, or have been, married to each other
- whether the parents live together. If so, where
- whether, to your knowledge, either of the parents have been involved in a Court case concerning a child. If so, give the date and name of the Court.

10.   The Family of the child(ren) (other children).

For any other child not already mentioned in the family (for example, a brother or a half sister) state

- the full name and address
- the date of birth (if known) or age
- the relationship of the child to you.

11.   Other adults.

State

- the full name, of any other adults (for example, lodgers) who live at the same address as any child named in paragraph 2
- whether they live there all the time
- whether, to your knowledge, the adult has been involved in a Court case concerning a child. If so, give the date and the name of the Court.

12.   Your reason(s) for applying and any plans for the child(ren).

State briefly your reasons for applying and what you want the Court to order.

- Do not give a full statement if you are applying for an order under Section 8 of Children Act 1989. You may be asked to provide a full statement later.
- Do not complete this section if this form is accompanied by a prescribed supplement.

13.   At the Court.

State

- whether you will need an interpreter at Court (parties are responsible for providing their own).
- whether disabled facilities will be needed at Court.

Signed   Date

GUARDIANSHIP AND WILLS

GUARDIANSHIP

It is very important to appoint a guardian or guardians for your children under 18. You should also appoint a substitute guardian who can act in the event that the primary guardian dies before you, and review the guardianship appointment from time to time to ensure that the appointed guardian is still able to take on the responsibility. Your partner or other person caring for your children will not automatically be deemed to be the guardian if you die.

Appointment of a guardian must be made in writing, signed and dated by the parent, and can be done in a will or separate document. It can be revoked in writing, provided it is signed and dated, even if it was first done as a clause in your will. This will serve as an expression of your wish and is not legally binding, but should the appointment be challenged, the court will take your wishes into account.

If you have not appointed a guardian, then anyone who has parental responsibility (PR) for the child will be entitled to be the guardian, or the court has the power to appoint one. In deciding any appointment it will consider the welfare of the child. However, this leaves the way open for maternal relatives, for example grandparents, to become involved. If a co-partner becomes a guardian on the death of the biological mother, she should appoint before the children are grown up.

Where a father shares PR

Where a biological mother has had children in marriage or where an unmarried father has acquired PR, the father automatically becomes the guardian on the mother's death, unless there is a residence order in place in favour of the mother or a co-parent. There have been cases where a father who had little contact or responsibility for the care of a child has removed her after the mother's death because of his automatic guardianship rights. It is possible for a co-parent to dispute his guardianship and apply for a residence order for the children herself. The courts will consider the welfare of the child, in particular how long they have been living with the co-parent and their own wishes, and may decide that the children are settled and should not be moved.

Where there is no father with PR

Where a biological mother has not been married to the father – for example, where a child has been born through self-insemination with a known donor – unless the donor has already acquired PR he would need to apply to the court for guardianship. Where the mother has already appointed a co-parent as a guardian, it is unlikely that the donor would obtain guardianship rights, particularly if he has had no involvement with the child. If a child has been born through anonymous donor insemination via a clinic, there is no problem in appointing a co-parent as the child's guardian.

MAKING A WILL

For lesbian mothers one of the most important aspects of making a will is to appoint a guardian for her children. It is also important to ensure that any money or property you have goes into the right hands.

If you are still legally married and you die without making a will, your property may go to your husband. If not, it will go to your children and there will be no provision for any lover, friend or co-parent.

Whether or not you have made a will and you were contributing towards your lover or friend and/or her child's maintenance, they may have a claim over any money or property you leave. Likewise if your lover or friend dies without leaving a will you may have a claim over her money or property, but these claims are complicated and legal fees could be substantial, so it is best to ensure that everyone makes a will.

Other provisions to consider in making a will include the following.

Executors and trustees

You should appoint executors for your will who agree to deal with the administration of your estate after your death. If any of your beneficiaries (people to whom you will leave property under your will) are less than 18 years old, you should appoint two executors who will also be trustees. Any property left to your children will be held in trust for them and managed by the trustees. It may be a good idea to appoint the guardians you wish to appoint to the trustees in this case.

Powers of executors or trustees

These are limited by law and it may be appropriate for them to be extended by various provisions in your will. These provisions may, in particular, extend the limited powers that trustees have to invest the monies in your estate and to borrow monies, insure property and advance monies to any child or children for their maintenance, education and general benefit.

Specific gifts and legacies

You should decide whether there are any specific items of your personal possessions that you wish to give to particular individuals or whether there are specific gifts of money you wish to leave. These gifts will be made before the division of the remainder of your estate, known as the 'residue', amongst your main or 'residuary' beneficiaries.

Remainder of your estate

Once any debts, tax, administration costs and funeral expenses have been paid and all your specific gifts have been made, the remainder of your estate will go to the people you have named as your residuary beneficiary or beneficiaries. You may wish to name one or more individuals or your children or a combination of both as your residuary beneficiary or beneficiaries. To deal with the possibility that both your partner and your beneficiaries predecease you, your will should include substitutes.

You can draw up a will using a standard form from a stationer's, but if you do not follow the correct procedure it will be invalid. It is probably best, particularly when providing for children, to get legal advice in drafting your will. Legal aid is available for the preparation of a will if you qualify on financial grounds and you are a single mother making a will to appoint a guardian for your child.

Once you have made your will, make sure it is kept in a safe place. You can keep it with other important papers, deposit it with your bank or solicitors for a fee, or deposit it with the Probate Registry for a fee of just £1. Wherever you decide to keep it, make sure you tell your executors.

APPENDIX C

YOUR MATERNITY RIGHTS

This is a brief outline of your maternity rights. For more details, contact Maternity Alliance or refer to *Maternity Rights* by Camilla Palmer (Legal Action Group in association with Maternity Alliance, London, 1996) (see Resources).

ANTENATAL CARE

As a pregnant employee you are entitled to paid time off during working hours for antenatal or pre-birth care, irrespective of your length of service or the hours you work.

MATERNITY LEAVE

All pregnant employees are entitled to a minimum 'general maternity leave' period. If you are in work while you are pregnant you are entitled to 14 weeks maternity leave, regardless of the number of hours you work per week or how long you have worked with your current employer. You need to write to your employers at least 21 days before you start your maternity leave, informing them that you are pregnant, giving them the expected date of childbirth and requesting that you are paid Statutory Maternity Pay (SMP) (see below).

You must tell your employers the date when you intend to start your maternity leave. The earliest you can start your maternity leave is 11 weeks before the expected week of childbirth. You can work right up to the expected week of childbirth except if you have a pregnancy-related illness or absence during the last six weeks of pregnancy or if the baby is born prematurely, in which case leave will start immediately.

EXTENDED MATERNITY ABSENCE

If you have worked for the same employer for two years at the beginning of the 11th week before the expected week of childbirth, you are entitled to return to work up to 29 weeks after the beginning of the week in which the baby was born. The period of extended maternity absence runs from the end of the 14-week maternity leave period and lasts up to 29 weeks after the beginning of the week of the birth.

RETURNING TO WORK

If you are returning to work at the end of 14 weeks' maternity leave, you do not need to give any notice of return – you can simply turn up at work at the end of your leave. If you want to return to work earlier, you must give seven days' notice in writing of the date you will return to your employers. The law does not allow you to work for two weeks after childbirth or, if you work in a factory, you are not allowed to work within four weeks of the birth.

If you have been on extended maternity absence and if you intend to return to work after your baby's birth, you must give your employer notice of this 21 days before you start your 14 weeks' maternity leave. If your employer makes a written request – not earlier than 21 days before the end of your maternity leave period – for confirmation that you intend to return to work, you must provide written confirmation within 14 days of receiving the request.

STATUTORY MATERNITY PAY (SMP)

There is no entitlement to full pay during maternity leave or absence, unless your contract provides for it. While on maternity leave you are entitled to either SMP or maternity allowance.

You can get SMP – a weekly payment for women employed during pregnancy – even if you do not plan to go back to work. SMP amounts to 90 per cent of your average pay for the first six weeks, after which you get the basic rate for up to 12 weeks of £54.55 per week.

To find out if you are entitled to SMP, contact your social security office, Citizen's Advice Bureau or law centre. SMP is paid for up to 18 weeks from whenever you leave work. The earliest you can get it, however, is 11 weeks before the birth of your baby. SMP will be paid by your employers in the same way that you are usually paid.

MATERNITY ALLOWANCE

You can get Maternity Allowance – a weekly allowance paid by the Benefits Agency for women who work just before or during their pregnancy but who can't get SMP – if you are self-employed or if you gave up work or changed jobs during your pregnancy. For example, you might not be entitled to SMP if you have recently changed jobs, become self-employed or have given up work. You will need to have worked and paid full-rate National Insurance contributions for at least 26 of the 66 weeks before the week the baby is due in order to qualify for maternity allowance. Your claim for Maternity Allowance – form MA1 – should be made as soon as possible after the 26th week of pregnancy. The allowance will not be paid before the 11th week of pregnancy and is paid for 18 weeks.

There are two rates. The higher rate (£54.44 in 1996/97) is paid to women who are employed in the 15th week before the expected week of childbirth, and the lower rate (£47.55) is paid to women who are self-employed or unemployed in the 15th week.

You may be entitled to other benefits, for example income support, incapacity benefit, housing benefit, council tax benefit or maternity expenses payment.

PREGNANCY-RELATED DISMISSAL

It is automatically unfair for your employers to dismiss you or select you for redundancy for any reason connected with pregnancy, childbirth or maternity leave. A dismissal which is automatically unfair will generally also be discriminatory.

You must lodge your claim with an industrial tribunal within three months of dismissal. Seek legal advice from your trade union, Lesbian and Gay Employment Rights (LAGER), citizens advice bureau or law centre, as the law is complicated.

CASE REFERENCES AND
LAW REPORTS

AN EXAMPLE OF CASE REFERENCES

For example:
Re H (a minor) (1993) 2 FLR 541.

Re H (a minor)	This refers to the name of the case
1993	The date of the case
2	The volume no. of the law report which the case is reported in
FLR	The name of the law report the case is reported in (see below for explanation of abbreviations)
541	The page the case is reported on

Some of the most common abbreviations used in this context are:

FCR	Family Court Reporter
FLR	Family Law Reports
Fam Law	Family Law (a journal)

INFORMATION ON LAW REPORTS

Law reports are published reports of the decisions of courts and tribunals and the reasons given for the decisions. Some cases are not reported, but these are sometimes written up in law journals such as *Family Law*.

Law reports are not easily available. Some central libraries have them in their reference sections. Some areas have law libraries run by their local Law Societies. Otherwise university or polytechnic libraries may have them, particularly if they run law courses. Many solicitors and law centres have at least some law reports.

LESBIAN PARENTING CASES

B v B (minors) (custody, care and control) (1991) 1 FLR 402
C v C (a minor) (custody: appeal) (1991) 1 FLR 223
C v C (custody of child) (no. 2) (1992) 1 FCR 206
Re C (a minor) (residence order: lesbian co-parents) (1994) *Fam Law* 468
E v E 27 November 1980 unreported
G v D 16 February 1983 unreported
Re H (a minor) (s. 37 direction) (1993) 2 FLR 541
Re P (a minor) (custody) (1983) 4 FLR 401
S v S (custody of children) (1978) 1 FLR 143
W v W 17 June 1980 unreported

BIBLIOGRAPHY

Akanke, 'Black in the Closet' in D Epstein, ed, *Challenging Lesbian and Gay Inequalities in Education*, Open University Press, Buckingham, 1994

Allen, Sue and Lynne Harne, 'Lesbian Mothers: The Fight for Child Custody' in B Cant and S Hemmings, eds, *Radical Records*, Routledge, London, 1988

Bainham, A, *Children and the New Law: The Children Act 1989*, Family Law, London, 1990

Bell, AP and MS Weinberg, *Homosexualities: A Study of Diversity Among Men and Women*, Simon & Schuster, New York, 1978

Bhabha, J and S Shutter, *Women's Movement: Women under Immigration and Refugee Law*, Trentham Books, Staffs, 1994

Brophy, Julia, 'Custody Law: Childcare and Inequality' in C Smart and S Sevenhuijsen, eds, *Child Custody and the Politics of Gender*, Routledge, London, 1989

Cretney, Stephen Michael, *Principles of Family Law*, third edition, Sweet & Maxwell, London, 1979

Department of Health, *Family Placements* vol 3 (1991)

Finkelor, D and D Russell, 'Women as Perpetrators' in D Finkelor, ed, *Child Sexual Abuse: New Theory and Research*, Free Press, New York, 1984

Golombok, Susan, Ann Spencer and Michael Rutter, 'Children in Lesbian and Single-Parent Households: Psychosexual and Psychiatric Appraisal', *Journal of Child Psychology and Psychiatry* 124, 4 (1983), pp551–72

Golombok, Susan and Fiona Tasker, 'Children in Lesbian and Gay Families: Theories and Evidence', *Annual Review of Sex Research* 5 (1994), pp73–100

——, 'Do Parents Influence the Sexual Orientation of Their Children? Findings from a Longitudinal Study of Lesbian Families', *Development Psychology* 32, 1 (1996), pp3–11

Golombok, Susan, Fiona Tasker and Clare Murray, 'Children Raised in Fatherless Families from Infancy: Family Relationships and the Socioemotional Development of Children of Lesbian and Single Heterosexual Women', *Journal of Child Psychology and Psychiatry*, in press

Gottman, JS, 'Children of Gay and Lesbian Parents' in FW Bozett and MB Sussman, eds, *Homosexuality and Family Relations*, Harrington Park Press, New York, 1990

Green, Richard, 'Sexual Identity of 37 Children Raised by Homosexual or Transsexual Parents', *American Journal of Psychiatry* 135, 6 (1978), pp692–7

Green, Richard, et al, 'Lesbian Mothers and their Children: A Comparison with Solo Parent Heterosexual Mothers and their Children', *Archives of Sexual Behavior* 15, 2 (1986), pp166–84

Harne, Lynne and Jill Radford, 'The Politics of the Family and the New Legislation' in Audrey Mullender and Rebecca Morley, eds, *Children Living with Domestic Violence: Putting Men's Abuse of Women on the Childcare Agenda*, Whiting and Birch, London, 1994

Hester, Marianne and Lorraine Radford, *Domestic Violence and Child Contact Arrangements in England and Denmark*, Polity Press, Bristol, 1996

Hoeffer, B, 'Children's Acquisition of Sex-Role Behavior in Lesbian-Mother Families', *American Journal of Orthopsychiatry* 5 (1981), pp536–44

Huggins, SL, 'A Comparative Study of Self-Esteem of Adolescent Children of Divorced Lesbian Mothers and Divorced Heterosexual Mothers' in FW Bozett, ed, *Homosexuality and the Family*, Harrington Park Press, New York, 1989

Kirkpatrick, Martha, 'Clinical Implications of Lesbian

Mother Studies', *Journal of Homosexuality* 13 (1987), pp201–11

Kirkpatrick, Martha, et al, 'Lesbian Mothers and Their Children: A Comparative Study', *American Journal of Orthopsychiatry* 51 (1981), pp545–51

Land, Hilary, 'Families and the Law' in John Muncie, et al, eds, *Understanding the Family*, Sage, London, 1995

Langford, Diane and A Pfeffercorn, 'Sex Education: Who Needs It?' in *Challenging Heterosexism*, GEN (March 1987)

Lesbian mother (anonymous), 'A Case of Heads He Wins – Tails She Loses', *Family Law Journal* 6 (1976), p230

Miller, JA, et al, 'The Child's Home Environment for Lesbian vs Heterosexual Mothers: A Neglected Area of Research', *Journal of Homosexuality* 7 (1981), pp49–56

Mucklow, BM and GK Phelan, 'Lesbian and Traditional Mothers' Responses to Child Behavior and Self-concept', *Psychological Reports* 44 (1979), pp880–82

Mullender, Audrey and Rebecca Morley, eds, *Children Living with Domestic Violence: Putting Men's Abuse of Women on the Childcare Agenda*, Whiting and Birch, London, 1994

National Council for Civil Liberties, *Section 28: A Practical Guide to the Law and its Implications*, NCCL, London, 1989

Pagelow, MD, 'Heterosexual and Lesbian Single Mothers: A Comparison of Problems, Coping and Solutions', *Journal of Homosexuality* 5 (1980), pp198–204

Patterson, Charlotte, 'Children of the Lesbian Baby Boom' in Beverly Greene and Gregory M Herek, eds, *Contemporary Perspectives on Gay and Lesbian Psychology: Theory, Research and Applications*, Sage, Beverly Hills, California, 1991

Patterson, Charlotte, 'Children of Lesbian and Gay Parents', *Child Development* 63 (1992), pp1025–42

Pennington, S, 'Children of Lesbian Mothers' in FW Bozett, ed, *Gay and Lesbian Parents*, Praeger, New York, 1987

Pies, C, *Considering Parenthood*, Spinsters Book Company, San Francisco, 1988

Radford, Jill, 'Policing Male Violence – Policing Women' in J Hanmer and M Maynard, eds, *Women, Violence and Social Control*, Macmillan, London, 1985

Radford, J, 'History of Women's Liberation Movements in Britain: A Reflective Personal History', in Griffin, et al, eds, *Stirring It: Challenges for Feminism*, Taylor and Francis, London, 1995

Radford, Lorraine, 'Domestic Violence, Child Contact and Mediation', *Rights of Women Bulletin* (Autumn 1994)

Rafkin, L, ed, *Different Mothers: Sons and Daughters of Lesbians Talk about their Lives*, Cleis Press, Pittsburgh, 1990

Rickford, F, 'Fostering with Pride', *Social Work Today* 23, 37 (May 1992), pp12–14

Rights of Women, *Lesbian Mothers on Trial: A Report on Lesbian Mothers and Child Custody*, Rights of Women, London, 1984

Rights of Women, 'The Asylum and Immigration Bill', *Rights of Women Bulletin* (Spring 1993)

Rights of Women Lesbian Custody Group, *Lesbian Mothers' Legal Handbook*, The Women's Press, London, 1986

Rutter, Michael, 'Psychosexual Development' in Michael Rutter, ed, *Scientific Foundations of Development Psychiatry*, Heinemann Medical, London, 1980

Saffron, Lisa, *Challenging Conceptions: Planning a Family by Self-Insemination*, Cassell, London, 1994

Sclater, Shelley Day, 'Divorce Law Changes – The Psychology of Dispute Resolution', *Rights of Women Bulletin* (Summer 1995)

Shutter, S, *Immigration and Nationality Law Handbook*, Joint Council for the Welfare of Immigrants, London, 1995

Southall Black Sisters, 'Domestic Violence and Asian Women. A Collection of Reports and Briefings', Southall Black Sisters, London, 1993

Steel, Moira, 'Lesbian Custody Disputes and Court Welfare Reports', *Social Work Monographs*, University of East Anglia, Norwich, 1990

Stonewall Immigration Group, 'United Kingdom Immigration

Law and Rules as They Affect Same-Sex Couples', Stonewall, London, June 1996

——, 'Letter to Stonewall Immigration Group from Neil Amos, private secretary to Immigration Minister, 19 April, 1995' Stonewall, London, 1996

Tasker, Fiona and Susan Golombok, 'Children Raised by Lesbian Mothers: The Empirical Evidence', *Fam Law* 21 (1991), pp184–7

——, 'Adults Raised as Children in Lesbian Families', *American Journal of Orthopsychiatry* 65, 2 (April 1995), pp203–15

Tatchell, P, *Out in Europe: A Guide to Lesbian and Gay Rights in 30 European Countries*, Channel 4 Television, 1990

West, DJ, ed, *Homosexuality Reexamined*, Duckworth, London, 1977

RESOURCES

ADOPTION AND FOSTERING

Lesbian and Gay Adoption, Fostering and Parenting Network

c/o London Friend
86 Caledonian Road
London N1 9DN
Phone and fax: 0171 833 1674

Provides information on local authorities and voluntary agencies, and produces a pack specifically for potential lesbian and gay foster and adoptive parents.

National Foster Care Association

Leonard House
5-7 Marshalsea Road
London SE1 1EP
Phone: 0171 828 6266

Parents for Children
41 Southgate Road
London N1 3JP
Phone: 0171 359 7530

ARTIFICIAL INSEMINATION

British Pregnancy Advisory Service (BPAS)
London Office
11–13 Charlotte Street
London W1P 1HD
Phone: 0171 222 0985

British Pregnancy Advisory Service (BPAS)
Head Office
Austy Manor
Wootton Wawen
Solihull
West Midlands B95 6BX
Phone: 01564 793225

Human Fertilisation and Embryology Authority
Paxton House
30 Artillery Lane
London E1 7LS
Phone: 0171 377 5077

Provides lists of licensed IVF clinics and information on the legal aspects of fertility services.

CHILD ABUSE

Action Against Child Sexual Abuse
PO Box 9502
London N17 7BW
Phone: 0181 365 9382

Feminist campaigning group.

COUNSELLING

The Pink Practice
BCM Pink Practice
London WC1N 3XX
Phone: 0181 809 7218

A counselling service for lesbians and gay men. Individual counselling, couple counselling and family therapy.

Project for Advice, Counselling & Education (PACE)
34 Hartham Road
London N7 9JL

DIVORCE

Divorce forms can be obtained from your local county court or from the Principal Registry of the Family Division of the High Court, Somerset House, The

Further reading

Challenging Conceptions: Planning a Family by Self-Insemination by Lisa Saffron (Cassell, London, 1994)

Considering Parenthood by C Pies (Spinsters Book Company, San Francisco, 1988)

Local Authority Social Services Department
For help and information about child abuse, refer to your local telephone directory for the number of your local authority social services department.

Phone: 0171 700 1323
Fax: 0171 609 4909

Counselling for lesbians and gay men. Low-cost counselling and sliding scale for fees. Has list of counsellors for referrals.

Women's Therapy Centre
6 Manor Gardens
London N7 6LA
Phone: 0171 263 6200

Strand, London WC2. Courts, law centres and citizen's advice bureaux provide leaflets on how to apply for a divorce.
See also legal advice.

DOMESTIC VIOLENCE

London Women's Aid
52–54 Featherstone Street
London EC1Y 8RT
Phone: 0171 251 6537
Also 01956 507096

Contact for referral.

National Women's Aid
Phone: 0345 023468

This is a low-cost phone number.

Northern Ireland Women's Aid
129 University Street
Belfast BT7 1HP
Phone: 01232 331818

24-hour helpline.

Southall Black Sisters
52 Norwood Road
Southall
Middlesex UB2 4DW
Phone: 0181 571 9595
Fax: 0181 574 6781

Provides advice, support and counselling for Asian and African-Caribbean women and their children fleeing domestic violence. Campaigns to abolish the '12-month rule'.

Further reading

Lesbians Talk Violent Relationships by Joelle Taylor and Tracy Chandler (Scarlet Press, London, 1995)

GENERAL SUPPORT, ADVICE AND INFORMATION

Black Lesbian & Gay Centre
Room 113
5a Westminster Bridge Road
London SE1 7XW
Phone: 0171 620 3885

Advice, counselling and telephone helpline service for black lesbians and black gays.

Cardiff Friend
Phone: 01222 340101

Lesbian and gay helpline, support and counselling.

Edinburgh Lesbian Line
Phone: 0131 557 0751

Glasgow Lesbian Line
Phone: 0141 552 3355

International Lesbian Information Service
ILIS secretariat c/o COC
Nieuwezijds Voorburgwal 68-70
1012 SE Amsterdam
The Netherlands
Phone: 0031 20 6231192
Fax: 0031 20 6267795

Lesbian news from all around the world.

Irish Gay Helpline
The Secretary
PO Box BM IGH
London WC1N 3XX
Phone: 0181 983 4111

Mondays 7.30–10pm.

Jewish Lesbian & Gay Helpline
BM Jewish Helpline
London WC1N 3XX
Phone: 0171 706 3123

Lesbian Archive & Information Centre
c/o Glasgow Women's Library
109 Trongate
Glasgow G1 5HD
Phone: 0141 552 8345

Lesbian Information Service
PO Box 8
Todmorden
Lancashire OL14 5TZ
Phone and fax: 01706 817235

Lesbian research centre and welfare agency which provides support and information to individual lesbians, especially isolated lesbians, groups and organisations. Produces 'Lesbians Who Are Mothers' resource list.

London Lesbian Line
BM Box 1514
London WC1N 3XX
Phone: 0171 251 6911

Support, helpline and information.

Nottingham Lesbian Centre
c/o Women's Centre
30 Chaucer Street
Nottingham NG1 5LP
Phone: 0115 941 0652

Older Black Lesbians
c/o Older Lesbian Network
Phone: 0171 242 6050

Offers support for black lesbians.

Orientations
c/o London Friend
86 Caledonian Road
London N1 9DN
Phone: 0171 833 1674

Offers support for Asian lesbians.

Oxford Lesbian & Gay Centre
North Gate Hall
St Michael's Street
Oxford OX1 2DU
Phone: 01865 200249

Shakti
c/o London Friend
86 Caledonian Road
London N1 9DN
Phone: 0171 833 1674

Offers support for South Asian lesbians.

Women's Resource Centre
4 Wild Court
off Kingsway
London WC2B 4AU
Phone: 0171 405 4045

Women's Information and Referral Exchange (WIRE) helpline open Monday, Tuesday, Thursday and Friday 11am–4pm. Information, support and advice on practically any issue.

HEALTH

Association of Community Health Councils for England & Wales (ACHEW)
Earlsmead House
30 Drayton Park
London N5 1PB
Phone: 0171 609 8405

Has a list of local Community Health Councils. ACHEW is the consumer voice in the NHS.

GLADD Doctors and Dentists
PO Box 5606
London W9 1WL

Health Authorities
Health Authorities (HA) are responsible for primary care services – GPs, dentists, chemists. Contact the HA if you have a complaint about these services. HAs also keep information about local doctors and other health-care workers. The address is on your NHS medical card.

Health Information Service
Phone: 0800 665544

Free national phone line giving information on any NHS service.

Women and Health
4 Carol Street
London NW1 0HU
Phone: 0171 482 2786

Lesbian health day held last Friday of each month.

Women's Health
52–54 Featherstone Street
London EC1Y 8RT
Phone: 0171 251 6580
Fax: 0171 608 0928

Free helpline advice on any health-related issue Monday, Wednesday, Thursday and Friday 10am–4pm. Drop-in library. Publications on numerous health issues. Write or phone for details of the self-insemination support group which meets every two weeks. Referrals to other health centres and professionals.

Further reading

The Black Woman's Health Book – Speaking for Ourselves by Evelyn C White (Seal Press, Washington, 1990)
A book by and for black women about contemporary health issues.

HOUSING

Albert Kennedy Trust
Unit 305A
Hatton Square
16/16A Baldwin's Gardens
London EC1N 7RJ
Phone: 0171 831 6562

Provides supported lodgings for homeless and at-risk 16– 19-year-old lesbians and gay men. Recruits and trains lesbian and gay carer household and arranges placements. Prospective carers can be on both their and a local authority's list.

Holds national register of local authority-approved lesbian and gay foster carers.

Local Authority Homelessness Unit
For emergency housing, refer to local telephone directory for the number of your local authority homelessness unit.

Stonewall Housing Association
2a Leroy Business Centre
436 Essex Road
London N1
Phone: 0171 359 5767

IMMIGRATION

Joint Council for the Welfare of Immigrants (JCWI)
115 Old Street
London EC1V 9JR
Phone: 0171 251 8706
Fax: 0171 251 8707

Stonewall
16 Clerkenwell Close
London EC1R 0AA
Phone: 0171 336 8860
Fax: 0171 336 8864

Information on the immigration campaign to support lesbian and gay couples and other activities.

UK Immigrants' Advisory Service
7th Floor
Brettenham House
Savoy Street
London WC2
Phone: 0171 240 5176/7

Women Immigration and Nationality Group (WING)
c/o Joint Council for the Welfare of Immigrants
115 Old Street
London EC2
Phone: 0171 251 8706

LEGAL ADVICE

Children's Legal Centre
University of Essex
Wivenhoe Park
Colchester
Essex CO4 3SQ
Phone: 01206 873820

Provides advice on law and policy relating to children and young people and produces leaflets and a magazine.

Citizens Advice Bureaux, National Association of (NACAB)
Phone: 0171 833 2181

Phone national number for your nearest CAB office for advice and representation on a range of legal issues and welfare rights, including housing and immigration.

Family Rights Group
The Print House
18 Ashwin Street
London E8 3DL
Phone: 0171 249 0008
Fax: 0171 923 2683

Gay and Lesbian Legal Advice (GLAD)
2 Greycoat Place
London SW1 1SB
Phone: 0171 831 3535

Gay and Lesbian Policing (GALOP)
Unit 2G Leroy House
436 Essex Road

London N1 3QP
Phone: 0171 704 2040

Helps lesbians and gay men in dealing with the police.

Law centres
Phone: 0171 387 8570

Phone for your nearest law centre for advice and representation on legal issues, including housing and immigration.

Lesbian & Gay Employment Rights (LAGER)
Unit 1G Leroy House
436 Essex Road
London N1 3QP
Phone: 0171 704 6066
Fax: 0171 704 6067

Lesbian helpline 0171 704 6066.

Maternity Alliance
45 Beech Street
London EC2P 2LX
Phone: 0171 588 8582

National body campaigning for improvements in maternity services. Information, leaflets in various languages, minicom.

National Council for One-Parent Families
255 Kentish Town Road
London NW5 2LX
Phone: 0171 267 1361

Rights of Women
52–54 Featherstone Street
London EC1Y 8RT
Fax: 0171 608 0928

Legal advice and support. Publications available.
Lesbian parenting line 0171 251 6576.
General advice line 0171 251 6577 open Tuesday, Thursday and Friday 12–2pm, Wednesday 3–5pm, Tuesday, Wednesday and Thursday evenings 7–9pm. Publications.

Further reading

Maternity Rights by Camilla Palmer (Legal Action Group in association with Maternity Alliance, London, 1996). Demystifies the law and addresses employment issues arising out of pregnancy and childbirth.

MEDIATION

National Family Mediation
9 Tavistock Place
London WC1H 9SN
Phone: 0171 383 5993

No known lesbian mediators employed. Will mediate between any two people.

PARENTING

Gay and Lesbian Parents Coalition International (GLPCI)
PO Box 43206
Montclair
New Jersey 07043
USA

Support group. Protects the rights of lesbian and gay parents and their children. Based in the USA, GLPCI monitors legislation, educates and operates annual summer camps for children.

Happy Families
PO Box 1060
Doncaster DN6 9QE
Phone: 01302 702601

Newsletter and networking for lesbian and gay families.

London Lesbian Parenting Group
c/o The Wheel
Wild Court off Kingsway
London WC2B 4AU

Support group.

Rights of Women Lesbian Parenting Line
Phone: 0171 251 6576

Stonewall Parenting Group
16 Clerkenwell Close
London EC1R 0AA
Phone: 0171 336 8860
Fax: 0171 336 8864

Meets monthly at The Link, near Camden Town, London, on alternate Saturday and Sunday afternoons. Meetings open to anyone interested in parenting issues. First part of the meeting is social. Children are welcome. Organises social activities for lesbian and gay parents.

Further reading

Asha's Mums by Rosamund Elwin and Michele Paulse (Women's Press, Toronto, Canada, 1990)
For young children, featuring lesbian mothers.

Heather Has Two Mommies by Lesléa Newman (in other words publishing, Northampton, Massachusetts, 1989).
Featuring lesbian parents; also mentions donor insemination.

Lesbian Lifestyles: Women's Work and the Politics of Sexuality by Gillian A Dunne (Macmillan Press, Ltd, Basingstoke, 1997)

Lesbians Talk Detonating the Nuclear Family by Julia Brosnan (Scarlet Press, London, 1996)

Mothers and Their Children – A Feminist Sociology of Childrearing by Jane Ribbens (SAGE Publications, London, 1994)

What About the Children? by Lisa Saffron (Cassell, London, 1996)

GLOSSARY

Affidavit
A statement in writing and on oath to be used as evidence in court proceedings. The person making it swears it before a solicitor or court official.

AID
Artificial insemination by donor.

Anti-lesbianism
Attitudes and practices which give lesbianism a negative value; also refers to discrimination against lesbians.

Appellant
Someone who is appealing against a decision of the court.

Applicant
The person making the application.

Barrister
Also known as 'Counsel'. Represents people in court from the Magistrate's Court up to the House of Lords; can only work on the instruction of a solicitor and may only communicate with the client through or in the presence of a solicitor. A barrister works from an office known as 'chambers' together with a group of barristers and organised by one or more 'clerks'. A barrister often specialises in one area of law eg family law, commercial law.

Bisexual
Someone who relates sexually and emotionally to both sexes.

Care order
Court order giving a local authority most of the parents' legal rights over a child.

Chambers
Barrister's office.

In chambers
Court hearing held in private.

Common law
Judge-made law as it has evolved over the centuries in this country, as distinct from law made by Parliament.

Conciliation

This is not reconciliation. It is an attempt by the courts to resolve matters without the bitterness of a protracted hearing. The parties are seen by a court welfare officer or mediator and an attempt is made to come to an agreement. It is not essential for a party to attend a conciliation appointment, but the court should be informed in good time by that person or her solicitor that they will not be attending. Some judges threaten that if a party does not attend for conciliation then her case will be prejudiced. It should not be, and a judge should be challenged as to her/his reason for making such a comment (this is best done by a lawyer).

Conference

A meeting between someone who is taking legal action and their barrister. The person's solicitor or representative should be present and the meeting usually takes place in the barrister's office (chambers).

Consent order

This is an agreement reached by the parties and approved by the court. Approval is not always automatic. It is an order of the court and is therefore enforceable through the court.

Contact

The child's right to see a significant adult. Contact can be direct (face to face) or indirect (letters, phone calls, presents). *Direct contact* can be *staying* (overnight, weekend, holidays) or *visiting* (contact only during the daytime).

The current philosophy about children and their relationships with their parents is that they have the right to have a relationship with both; thus courts will bend over backwards to make contact work for a non-resident father. This philosophy can be used to the advantage of lesbian mothers, since children will inevitably have the right to contact with their mother (unless she has done something against the welfare of the child, such as physical abuse). Therefore the child will know that her mother is a lesbian, stay with her mother, have contact with her mother's partner and thus there is no reason why, ultimately, the mother should not have residence of the child.

County court

Deals with non-criminal matters only. It hears domestic violence cases, undefended divorces and related matters of maintenance, residence or contact and adoption.

Court of Appeal

Hears appeals from the High Court and County Court.

Court welfare officer (CWO)

A probation officer, or, in some parts of the country, a local authority social worker, who is appointed by the court to prepare a welfare report in cases involving children.

In many contested cases a CWO will be appointed. The CWO's job is to interview the parties, see the parties with the children (unless one party objects to that), see the children, and, if they are old enough, ascertain their views on the situation. Whether a child is old enough depends on the individual child, her understanding, intelligence, and ability to communicate. It could be as young as seven, it could be ten or eleven. A CWO's report will take at least twelve weeks to prepare. A CWO will not necessarily attend court; a specific request must be made to ensure her/his attendance. It is always worth asking a CWO whether she/he has prepared reports on cases involving lesbians before and whether she/he would be interested in seeing copies of the latest research on the children of lesbian mothers, recently completed by Susan Golombok and Fiona Tasker and published in *American Journal of Orthopsychiatry* (April 1995), p203. Their earlier work is published in 1991 *Fam Law* 21, pp184–7

Covenant
Legally binding agreement signed and witnessed. A person can covenant to pay money towards a child's maintenance and get tax relief.

Cross-examination
Questioning of someone in court by the barrister for the other side.

Decree absolute
Court order making a divorce final.

Decree nisi
First part of court order for divorce.

Defined access
Where the court lays down fixed times for contact visits.

Deported
Sent out of the country.

District judge
Sits in the County Court and Family Division of the High Court and is appointed by the Lord Chancellor; deals with procedural issues until the trial of a matter takes place, applications for maintenance of the spouse and other financial matters in divorce proceedings; deals with contact with children where the principle of contact is agreed and the only matter in dispute is the amount of contact; presides over conciliation appointments where there is a residence dispute.

Ex-parte
An application to the court by one party to proceedings without the other party having been given notice and therefore not being represented.

Expert witness
An 'expert' witness can give her/

his opinion on a subject within her/his expertise (eg a psychiatrist). This is an exception to the general rule that witnesses may only speak of facts which they themselves have observed and may not give their opinion on those facts.

Filing at court

Sending legal documents to the court.

Freeing order

An order declaring a child to be free for adoption.

Gender

As opposed to 'sex', 'gender' is a socially imposed division between women and men based on social, emotional and psychological attributes which a culture expects from either sex.

Gender roles

Developed by sociologists, gender roles are a way of describing the imposed different social roles expected of women and men.

Guardian ad litem

A person appointed by the court from an approved panel of social workers to act as the child's representative (sometimes together with a solicitor) in care proceedings.

Hearsay evidence

Evidence of a fact not actually perceived by a witness with one of her/his own senses, but said by her/him to have been stated by another person. The general rule is that such evidence cannot be used to prove the truth of a fact, but there are exceptions to this rule.

Heterosexism

A belief in the superiority of heterosexuality; policies and practices which serve to elevate heterosexuality and subordinate homosexuality.

Heterosexual

A person who relates sexually and emotionally to the opposite sex.

High court

Divided into three divisions. The Family Division deals with defended divorces and can decide on related questions of maintenance (for the spouse), residence and contact, wardship and adoption.

Homophobia

Fear, dislike, hatred of lesbians and gay men.

Homosexual

A person who relates sexually and emotionally to the same sex.

House of Lords

Hears appeals from the Court of Appeal but only with leave of either the Court of Appeal or the Appeals Committee of the House of Lords.

Illegitimate child

A child who is not born within marriage.

In the closet
Keeping your sexual identity secret.

Injunction
A court order requiring someone to do, or to stop doing, something.

Irrebuttable presumption
An assumption of the truth of a thing which the law will not allow to be contradicted by any counter-evidence.

Joint residence orders
These can be awarded to the adult carers who all live in the same house or to people who live apart – eg when a relationship between the adults has broken down and/or the adults wish to live apart.

Judicial separation
Legal separation of a married couple. The grounds are the same as for a divorce but after a judicial separation the parties remain legally married.

Judiciary
All judges, magistrates.

Juvenile
A person under the age of 17.

Juvenile Court
See Magistrate's Court.

Law report
A report of a court decision written up in the officially recognised legal reports, giving the facts of the case/reasons for the decision. Law reports are usually written by barristers.

Law Society
Association of solicitors which also administers legal aid.

Leave to appeal
Permission from the court to lodge an appeal against a decision of the court.

Legal aid
This is a scheme run by the Law Society and funded by public funds. It enables people whose income and capital do not exceed certain limits to have free legal advice and representation, provided the Law Society is satisfied that they have a case.

Lesbian
A woman who relates sexually and emotionally to other women.

Magistrate's Court
Deals with criminal, including juvenile, and non-criminal matters. Non-criminal matters include domestic violence, certain maintenance applications and residence or contact applications. Sitting as a juvenile court, the magistrates also hear care proceedings.

Maintenance
Regular payments of money paid from one spouse (usually the husband) to the other spouse either during or after marriage; or regular payments of money for a child paid by a parent (usually the father).

Matrimonial home
House in which wife and husband

live; or previously shared home of married couple.

Mediation

A process in which trained and impartial mediators assist those involved in relationship breakdown to communicate better with one another and to reach their own informed decisions about some or all of the related issues, for example arrangements for the children, their relationship, finance, property and other practical matters. Not appropriate where violence has been an issue in the relationship.

Mediator

A go-between (used in conciliation appointments and mediation sessions).

Minor

A person under the age of 18.

Next friend

Adult in whose name legal proceedings are taken on behalf of a child.

Non-molestation order

An order made by a court to a person ordering them not to pester, cause trouble, annoy or inconvenience a named person(s). Conduct causing trouble does not have to be violent.

Nuclear family

Wife, husband and children living together as a separate group.

Occupation order

Where an applicant who has an estate or interests or matrimonial home right, they may apply to the court for an order to enforce their entitlement to remain in occupation or, if the applicant is not so entitled, to restrict the respondent's entitlement to occupation.

Official Solicitor

Acts in High Court cases as the representative of a minor if the court decides that the minor needs independent representation.

On remand

In prison/custody awaiting trial.

Ouster Injunction

Court order directing someone (usually a man) to leave the home.

Parental responsibility (PR)

Entitles a person to be involved in major discussions and decisions about major matters in a child's life, such as school, religion and which country a child should live in. It has been held that PR means very little. In one case it was granted to a father who had absolutely no contact with a child, because the child was going to be placed for adoption, so that he would have the legal status to be a party in the adoption proceedings. Although PR follows automatically from the making of a residence order, in practice it has nothing to do with residence or contact. However, PR can be useful when dealing with doctors (signing for treatment, obtaining information) and schools (discussing a child's progress).

Parties
All the people who are entitled to be heard in the case, ie the Applicant and the Respondent. In a case involving a child born as a result of a heterosexual relationship the parties will usually be the mother and father. In a case involving a child born to lesbians the parties will usually be the non-biological mother – who will usually be the Applicant – and the biological mother – who will usually be the Respondent.

Pathological
Diseased.

Petitioner
Person who applies to the court for a divorce.

Place of Safety Order
A local authority or the police can, without notice to the parents, apply to a magistrate for an order that a juvenile be taken to a place of safety, eg a local authority children's home or foster-home, for a maximum period of 28 days.

Power of arrest
A power given to the police by a court to arrest a named person.

Precedent
A decision made by a previous court which can serve as a rule or pattern to be followed or considered in a subsequent case.

Probation officer
Person who works in conjunction with the courts and who often writes a report concerning the general welfare of someone coming before the court at the court's request.

Prohibited steps
This can be an order to stop either carer or a third party doing something detrimental to the child's interest, such as remove the child from the country, cut her hair or pierce her ears.

Psychiatrist
Doctor who studies and treats mental illness.

Psychoanalysis
A method for treating so-called 'mental disorders' by investigating interaction of unconscious and conscious elements of the mind.

Psychologist
Someone who tests and measures mental characteristics.

Psychosexual
A general term often used very loosely by psychologists and psychiatrists to describe a person's identity, development and behaviour, eg gender-role behaviour, sexual orientation (lesbian, gay, heterosexual) and gender identity.

Reasonable contact
Where contact is agreed between the parties without the court laying down specified times. What is reasonable depends on your point of view, and a woman may often be pressurised into agreeing

to contact arrangements which she finds unreasonable.

Registrar
Sits in the County Court and Family Division of the High Court and is appointed by the Lord Chancellor; deals with procedural issues until the trial of a matter takes place, applications for maintenance and other financial matters in divorce proceedings; deals with contact with children where the principle of contact is agreed and the only matter in dispute is the amount of contact; presides over conciliation appointments where there is a residence dispute.

Reported case
A case decision which has been written up in the law reports and which therefore can be quoted.

Residence
Awarded to the person with whom the child will live for most of the time. That person has responsibility for the day-to-day decisions about a child's life, for example bedtime, diet, activities. A person with residence can take the children out of the jurisdiction (ie to Scotland or abroad) for up to 28 days, without the agreement of any other person and without leave of the court.

Respondent
The person against whom legal action is being taken. The person who will receive notification of the application and will have the right to come to court to give her/his view and call evidence.

Rules of natural justice
The right to a fair and unbiased hearing.

Section 8 orders
Section 8 (of the Children Act 1989) orders may be made in most proceedings which specifically relate to the care and upbringing of children. They are designed to provide practical solutions to problems that arise. The overriding aim is to encourage adults to maintain their involvement in the child's life. A Section 8 order can be made at any time until the child's 18th birthday but only exceptionally once the child has reached the age of 16.

There are four types of Section 8 orders: contact orders, prohibited steps orders, residence orders and specific issue orders (see separate entries in Glossary for descriptions of these orders).

Sexual orientation
Defines a person's sexual identity.

SI
Self-insemination.

Solicitor
Can represent people in Magistrate's Courts, County Courts and sometimes in the Crown Court. Rarely represents a client in contested family matters but instead instructs a barrister. A solicitor deals direct with the client and is responsible for the preparation of

the case, which includes advising the client, interviewing witnesses and instructing a barrister.

Specific issue

This can require a carer or a third party to do something, eg ensure the child attends a doctor's appointment.

Statement of marital breakdown

A statement by one or both of the parties in a marriage that they believe the marriage has broken down. The maker(s) of the statement must be aware of the purpose of the period for reflection and consideration and they must have attended an information meeting not less than three months before making the statement (Family Law Act 1996).

Status quo

The current state of affairs; refers here to the current living arrangements of the child.

Statute

Law made by Parliament.

Statutory charge

Charge made by the Law Society for legal costs where property/money is involved.

Supervision order

A court order which gives the general supervision of a child to a local authority and which can last until the child is 18.

Undertaking

This is a promise to the court to do something. It has the same effect as an order and if it is broken a person may be committed to prison.

Variation

Court order changing an original court order.

Ward of court

A child who has been made a ward comes under the court's 'protection', ie all major decisions relating to the child have to be referred to the court for its approval. Since the Children Act 1989 came into effect, wardship is very rarely used.

Wardship proceedings

Legal action making a child a ward of court.

Welfare principle

Section 1 of the Children Act 1989 states that the welfare of the child shall be regarded as the first and paramount (ie supreme) consideration in any proceedings relating to children.

Welfare report

A report which may be, and frequently is, ordered by a district judge or judge in any proceedings involving children. It is prepared by a court welfare officer, who investigates the circumstances of any person claiming residence or contact and interviews the parties and the children. The report has to be shown to the parties to the proceedings.

INDEX